ESSENTIALS *for* EXCELLENCE

Connecting Sunday School to Life

Alan Raughton and Louis B. Hanks

Introduction by Gene Mims

SUNDAY SCHOOL PLANNER
AND CD-ROM

ISBN 0-6330-8918-4

This book is a resource in the Leadership and Skill Development category
of the Christian Growth Study Plan for course number
LS-0048.

Dewey Decimal Classification: 268.1
Subject Headings: SUNDAY SCHOOLS—ADMINISTRATION\PLANNING

Printed in the United States of America

Leadership and Adult Publishing
LifeWay Church Resources
One LifeWay Plaza
Nashville, Tennessee 37234-0175

To order additional copies of this book or other resources identified as available from
LifeWay Church Resources, WRITE LifeWay Church Resources Customer Service,
One LifeWay Plaza, Nashville, TN 37234-0113; FAX order to (615) 251-5933;
PHONE 1.800.458.2772; E-MAIL to CustomerService@lifeway.com;
ONLINE at *www.lifeway.com*; or visit the LifeWay Christian Store serving you.

Acknowledgements
Cover design: Jim Campbell

Gratitude is expressed to Topper Reid, Hunter Street Baptist Church, Hoover, Alabama,
and Ron Brown, LifeWay Church Resources, for their unique and visionary contributions
to this resource.

Scripture quotations marked (NIV) are from the Holy Bible, New International Version.
Copyright © 1973, 1978, 1984 by International Bible Society.

Scripture quotations marked HCSB® are taken from the *Holman Christian Standard Bible®*,
© copyright 1999, 2000, 2001, 2002, 2003 by Broadman & Holman Publishers.
Used by permission.

CONTENTS

HOW TO USE THIS RESOURCE

The premise of *Essentials for Excellence: Connecting Sunday School to Life* is that Sunday School is the foundational strategy for helping your church do the work of the Great Commission. Sunday School becomes the way to take the church's "Great Assignment" and break it down into manageable pieces. It is a way of involving people, using resources wisely, and multiplying efforts strategically. It is a way to turn your vision of what God wants your church to do into reality. As a result, this book can and should be used in meaningful ways throughout the year.

A Launch Event

A new year Launch becomes a time to celebrate past accomplishments, communicate future plans, train leaders, commission leaders for service, challenge the church about the potential of Sunday School strategy, and create a sense of excitement and purpose for the new church year. Elements of such an event might include:

• *A Sunday School rally*

A rally is for all Sunday School leaders. It may be a Friday evening kickoff for a weekend event. Elements might include a welcome and introduction of new leaders; dinner; celebration of past accomplishments; presentation of an annual theme, if used; overview of goals and action plans; an inspirational message; and other elements.

• *A leadership training event*

Training might be done on Saturday of a weekend event. Promote as a training spectacular that will equip all leaders to be more effective.

Training might include a general session with all leaders. During this time, the pastor, Sunday School director, or minister of education may overview the annual plan (unless done at the rally), review the organizational structure, preview the annual calendar, and so forth. The majority of time, however, needs to be spent in age-group leadership training. The age-group e-books and other items on this book's **CD-ROM** are to be used in such training.

The weekend excitement can continue with the Sunday morning worship. A well-planned emphasis can help focus on the work of the church and the calling of God's people to share the good news. Sunday School can be highlighted as the foundational strategy for leading people to faith in the Lord Jesus Christ and for building on-mission Christians through open Bible study groups.

Commissioning Sunday School leaders during the worship service can indicate the importance of the commitment leaders are making and can emphasize to the congregation the value the church places on ministries conducted through Sunday School. See the **CD-ROM** for a commissioning service/responsive reading.

Annual Planning

The evaluative information needed for annual planning is a major focus of Section 1 (pp. 13-49), as leaders assess their Sunday School vision. As a result, this process and the information obtained from various sources should precede annual planning. By beginning annual planning in the spring before a new year, new leaders can be enlisted and trained prior to beginning to serve.

Age-Group Training and Evaluation

While it is desirable for the entire Sunday School team to be in simultaneous training, separate age-group training can be offered to meet distinctive needs. If a Launch event for the entire team is not held, then encourage your age-group leaders to offer training for their team.

Often it is timely to offer training and evaluation in January or the spring of the year. This schedule gives new leaders time to understand their roles and all leaders, a chance to identify additional training needs. This resource, especially its age-group content, is designed to be used anytime during the year.

One-on-One Mentoring or Personal Development

Still another use is to offer this book or its CD-ROM material to leaders who will read or do activities on their own time. Ask for responses back within a reasonable time, and encourage leaders to request Christian Growth Study Plan credit.

If you are the leader who purchased this combination book and CD-ROM, do not keep its information to yourself! Download files for age-group leaders; share the CD so they may do so; highlight information—get the word out to your entire team and expect the results of everyone sharing the same vision!

Connecting Sunday School to Life

CD-ROM Contents

Preschool Sunday School Ministry
- E-book: *Essentials for Excellence: Connecting Preschool Sunday School to Life*
- E-book additional resources (16)
- E-book 2 1/2-hour teaching plan
- Teaching plan resources (23)

Children's Sunday School Ministry
- E-book: *Essentials for Excellence: Connecting Children's Sunday School to Life*
- E-book additional resources (9)
- E-book 2 1/2-hour teaching plan
- Teaching plan resources (10, including PowerPoint® presentation)

Student Sunday School Ministry
- E-book: *Essentials for Excellence: Connecting Student Sunday School to Life*
- E-book 2 1/2-hour teaching plan
- E-book additional resources (17)
- Teaching plan resources (5, including PowerPoint® presentation)

Adult Sunday School Ministry
- E-book: *Essentials for Excellence: Connecting Adult Sunday School to Life*
- E-book additional resources (29)
- E-book 2 1/2-hour teaching plan
- Teaching plan resources (16, including PowerPoint® presentation)

Special Education Ministry
- E-Book: *Essentials for Excellence: Connecting Special Education Sunday School to Life*
- E-book 2 1/2-hour teaching plan
- E-book additional resources: articles (27), forms (9), handouts (14) for use with e-book or teaching plan; includes 2 PowerPoint® presentations

FAITH Sunday School Ministry
- E-book: *Essentials for Excellence: Connecting FAITH Sunday School to Life*

General Leadership
- Sunday School Definition
- Overview of Ten Best Practices
- Sunday School Growth and Evaluation Plan Summary Sheet
- Meeting Space Specifications Chart
- Recommended Equipment and Furnishings by Age Group
- Evaluation Worksheets
- Benefits of Annual Planning
- Sample Strategic Plan Sheet
- Grouping by Age Groups
- Article: Strategic Use of Multiple Meeting Times
- A Model Enlistment Visit
- Confidential Volunteer Screening Form
- Prepared by God to S.E.R.V.E.
- Suggested Monthly Planning Team Meeting Agenda
- Team Roster
- Leadership Position Descriptions
- *Weekly Leadership Meeting items:* Benefits, Content, Possible Schedules, Sunday School Director's Role, Pastor's Role, How to Start, How to Keep Going
- Sunday School Leader and Member Training Survey
- LifeWay Curriculum Characteristics
- Benefits of Using LifeWay Sunday School Resources
- Launch commissioning service

Interactive forms
- Sunday School Strategy Growth Worksheet
- Budget Planning Sheet
- Streaming video

Links are also given to appropriate LifeWay.com sources of information.

INTRODUCTION

Sunday School as a Biblical Model for Leaders

God wants our Bible study ministries to succeed. I cannot imagine any leader thinking that the Lord would send His Son to die for the world's sins, offer salvation and forgiveness to anyone who trusts in Him, and establish the church on earth—to ensure failure! Know that success is the design for Sunday School ministry and the philosophy behind resources like this one. Also know that success can happen through your leadership.

Understanding the purpose and principles of Sunday School ministry will help to ensure success. To come to these realizations is especially important if you are in a Sunday School that is not as successful as you think it can be. If you face constant burdens of leadership training, recruitment, worker retention, curriculum decisions, space adjustments, and commitment (or lack thereof), then you have come to the right resource for help.

Begin your journey, however, by looking at the big picture. Before you and other leaders get busy and start "doing things," be sure to get the right view of what you have with its potential.

Sunday School ministry is unparalleled in potential impact. Its scope, power, and effectiveness are unprecedented in reaching people for Christ, assimilating them into a local church, discipling them, and seeing believers transformed into Christlikeness. With a tool like Sunday School ministry, you have something few believers have or can ever experience: the opportunity and resources to be a part of something great in the kingdom of God.

The Great Commission

The evidence is in, and the verdict is clear: The average church in America does not have a clear strategy for reaching the lost in their communities. The lack of evangelism strategies for training and witnessing and the absence of clearly defined discipleship ministries show that many of our churches are busy doing other things—not the one thing the Lord commanded us.

Connecting Sunday School to Life

The Great Commission is simple. We are to make disciples. We are to present the good news of Christ and of God's kingdom, asking people to repent of their sins and trust Christ for forgiveness and eternal life. We are to baptize them, immersing them in water in the name of the Father, Son, and Holy Spirit. We are to teach them to obey the things Christ has taught us in His Word.

The population of the United States continues to grow, but our churches are not keeping pace with population growth. The Great Commission is the answer our churches desperately need today. We must view persons who are apart from Christ through the lens of the Great Commission. If we see people as either lost without Christ or as believers in Christ, then decision-making in the church gets much easier. We will know what to do and why. We will be freed from the traps of busyness to focus on the right things.

From the life of Christ, we see the biblical principles of making disciples, maturing disciples, and multiplying disciples into Great Commission ministries. One of the methods Jesus used in His kingdom ministry was that of small groups. He used two different kinds of small groups effectively. One was open to anyone who was seeking the Lord. The other was restricted to His disciples for training and equipping.

The open group is a foundational strategy for any church that is truly seeking to fulfill the Great Commission. Look at the following description: *An open-group strategy exists to lead people to faith in the Lord Jesus Christ and to build on-mission Christians by engaging people in foundational evangelism, discipleship, fellowship, ministry, and worship through ongoing, evangelistic Bible study units of believers together with unbelievers in an atmosphere of compassion to share the gospel.*[1]

This definition captures the essence of Sunday School and its effectiveness in helping a church fulfill the Great Commission. A Sunday School class is an effective Great Commission unit because it contains everything necessary to fulfill that command. It has evangelism, discipleship, fellowship, ministry, and is married to the morning worship service. In addition, Sunday School ministry enables these important biblical functions to be done by individuals in and through a group.

Sunday School is a small-group strategy that allows believers and unbelievers to come together around Bible study and fellowship with an evangelistic focus. It is a most efficient way to reach people for Christ. With the Bible as its curriculum and evangelism, edification, fellowship, and assimilation as its focus, Sunday School as an open-group strategy is a key element in a church's overall vision of doing God's will.

Sunday School and Other Church Ministries

"How," you might ask, "does Sunday School fit with the rest of our church's ministries?" That is a great question, and I can best answer it by outlining what the New Testament says.

The Great Commission is the single focus and vision of every church in the kingdom of God. We never have to create a compelling image of an achievable future for our churches because Christ gave it to us in Matthew 28:19-20. The biblical principles of how to fulfill the Great Commission are sprinkled throughout the New Testament but specifically in Acts 2. While we do not need to read all of Peter's sermon or its results, reading part of it now is helpful.

Peter's famous sermon at Pentecost is a gospel sermon. He urged people to repent of their sins and trust Christ. Luke (who wrote Acts) concluded the passage by giving the results of the day.

> So those who <u>accepted his message</u> were baptized, and that day about three thousand people were added to them. And they devoted themselves to <u>the apostles' teaching</u>, <u>to fellowship</u>, to the breaking of bread, and to prayers.
>
> Then fear came over everyone, and many wonders and signs were being performed through the apostles. Now all the believers were together and had everything common. So they <u>sold their possessions and property and distributed the proceeds to all, as anyone had a need</u>. And every day they <u>devoted themselves to meeting together in the temple complex</u>, and broke bread from house to house. They ate their food with gladness and simplicity of heart, praising God and having favor with all the people. And every day the Lord added those being saved to them (Acts 2:41-47, HCSB).

How did the early church fulfill the Great Commission? In the presence and power of the Holy Spirit, they <u>evangelized</u>, <u>discipled</u>, <u>fellowshipped</u>, <u>ministered</u>, and <u>worshiped</u> together. These five biblical functions are crucial and indispensable to a church's work. And guess what? Sunday School fulfills every one of those functions. That means that you have through your Sunday School ministry everything you need to obey the Lord and fulfill His Commission.

A Sunday School strategy that intentionally includes each of these functions will not fail. It cannot because it is a strategy born and sustained by the Holy Spirit. <u>But what results can you expect?</u> Four are described in the New Testament.

Connecting Sunday School to Life

You can expect *numerical growth*: "Believers were added to the Lord in increasing numbers" (Acts 5:14, HCSB). You will have *spiritual growth*: "And they devoted themselves to the apostles' teaching" (Acts 2:42, HCSB). You will have *growth in ministries* in your church: "So they sold their possessions and property and distributed the proceeds to all, as anyone had a need" (Acts 2:45, HCSB).

Finally, you will see your church *advance the kingdom of God* as Jesus prophesied: "But you will receive power when the Holy Spirit has come upon you, and you will be My witnesses in Jerusalem, in all Judea and Samaria, and to the ends of the earth" (Acts 1:8, HCSB).

Do you feel the excitement of what Sunday School can and should be, of how God uses it to accomplish His purposes in the world? Now think for a moment: *you are a part of this great movement.* You are a leader in a Great Commission enterprise!

I hope you develop this kingdom vision for your Sunday School, and I urge you to develop a strategy with your Sunday School leaders to take fullest advantage of what the Lord has given you. You have the most powerful and effective Bible study ministry possible to fulfill the Great Commission.

As you read or teach this book, this is an excellent opportunity to examine your Sunday School and to determine why you are doing ministry. Ask yourself whether the way you currently do Sunday School will allow your church to fulfill the Great Commission. Evaluate your church's commitment to Sunday School ministry and to its effectiveness.

I pray that the future will be bright as you lead God's people to be their best as on-mission Christians who are doing God's will and are celebrating His kingdom.

[1]Gene Mims, *Kingdom Principles of Church Growth, Revised and Expanded* (Nashville: LifeWay Press, 2001), 102.

SECTION 1

How's Your Sunday School Vision?

A high school baseball player stepped into the batter's box. It was the bottom of the tenth inning of a tie game. One parent turned to the batter's father and said, "I have a vision of him hitting a home run." Even as they laughed, the batter drove the pitch over the fence to win the game. The two men cheered with delight, celebrating together a vision that had become reality.

A young couple stood proudly in their newly remodeled home. It was everything they had envisioned during long months of planning and labor. But they didn't stop to revel too long, for they already were starting to think about the landscaping project that was next on their list.

Holding her graduate degree in her hand, the woman sat in quiet reflection. Many nights over the past several years, she had tucked the children into bed and, though weary, had gone to the kitchen table to continue preparation for classes the next day. It had taken a long time, but she had reached her divinely inspired goal. But this was not the end; it was only the beginning. She wanted to apply what she had achieved in such a way as to carry out faithfully what she believed was God's purpose for her life.

Identifying the Vision

What Is Vision?

To some people a vision is a wish. Any connection between the wish and the reality is a surprising coincidence, much like the batter's home run. In this case, the parent's vision had nothing to do with the batter's skill.

To others vision is a dream. Commitment, diligence, drive, and hard work connect the dream and the reality. Like the young couple in the second example, these individuals plan their vision or series of visions. When one dream is accomplished, these folk move quickly to another one. In a sense, such people thrive on making what they have seen in their mind's eye into what they and others can see with their physical eyes.

For those who are like the woman in the third example, vision is a spiritual experience. The connector between vision and reality is a deep and personal relationship with God. A vision is something for which a person strives in order to be better equipped for service to God and to others. In essence, vision is from God.

Simply stated, vision may be defined as a preferred or desired future reality. Well, so are wishes and dreams, are they not? Yes, that is what the three words hold in common, but significant differences exist. A wish is a desire that is generally regarded as unattainable. A dream is a desire that often is considered too good to be true. More often than not, wishes and dreams remain just that.

The vision we will consider throughout this book is a compelling image of an achievable future. "A vision, while also a desired future reality . . . is a desire that captures the heart and mind and coalesces the resources of the group toward whatever action is necessary to cause the vision to become a concrete reality."[1] An individual or a group is so possessed by such a vision that action is inevitable, not optional.

Why Is Vision Important?

A buzzword refers to an important-sounding or technical word or phrase that is used to impress others. *Vision* has the potential to be one of those words. Just talking about vision and writing vision statements are not enough. Vision is not vision if it does not lead to action—but not just any action.

The actions that come from vision are planned, intentional, and focused. That is why vision is so important. It gives intention and direction both to our planning and to what we do.

What Is the Source of This Compelling Vision?

From what source does such a vision come? Or perhaps the better question is, From what source *should* such a vision come?

As believers and followers of Christ, called of God to leadership roles in His church, our vision should come from God. The vision we have for ourselves and our churches is to be an expression of our knowledge and understanding of God's vision. Our vision is what God desires for me and my church, you and your church, to become.

We come to know and understand that vision through our relationship with Him. The closer we are to Him, the better able we are to know and understand His aspirations for us.

The Bible is filled with examples of faithful people for whom God had a vision. Out of their relationship with Him, His vision became their vision. That vision moved them to action that resulted in the fulfillment of God's purposes.

Consider on the next few pages the examples provided by Moses, Nehemiah, Jesus, and Paul. For each:

> • *Identify a defining moment in that person's relationship with God, a moment that led to his knowing and understanding God's vision.*
>
>
> • *Ask and answer, What was the vision?*
>
>
> • *Ask and answer, What actions were taken to make the vision reality?*
>
>
> • *Ask and answer, What were the outcomes?*

Moses (Ex. 3–4)	**Nehemiah** (Neh. 1–6)
A Defining Moment	A Defining Moment
The Vision	The Vision
Actions	Actions
Outcomes	Outcomes
Jesus (Luke 2:41-50; Matt. 3:13-17)	**Paul** (Acts 9:1-31)
A Defining Moment	A Defining Moment
The Vision	The Vision
Actions	Actions
Outcomes	Outcomes

Connecting Sunday School to Life

To Whom Does a Vision Belong?
Now look at your answers and note some similarities.
- The vision of God for Moses was to deliver a people from bondage and establish a nation (Ex. 3).
- The vision of God for Nehemiah was to rebuild the city wall (Neh. 2).
- The vision of God for Jesus, His Son, was to establish the rule and reign (kingdom) of God (Luke 2:49; Matt. 4:17).
- The vision of God for Paul was to spread the gospel to the nations (Acts 9:15).

Whose vision did each person have? *God* instilled a vision in the heart of His chosen servant for an appointed time. What did He expect? *God* expected each of His servants to act on His vision to achieve His purpose through His power for His glory. Anything less would not be God-sized, God-given, or God-honoring. In turn, each leader cast the vision to another. Those who caught the vision became involved in acting on it and in helping cast the vision to other people.

Making a Personal Connection: What Does All This Mean to Me?

Let's start pulling some of this together to help you assess the state of your church and its Sunday School ministry in particular.[2] Does *your church* have a God-given vision of what can be accomplished through its Sunday School ministry? For our purposes let's call that statement a *Sunday School vision*. What is your perception of the congregation's Sunday School vision?

Consider four dimensions (introduced in pp. 8-11) in which God desires for growth to take place or kingdom results to be achieved. Your Sunday School ministry can be a strategic methodology to accomplish these outcomes.

Numerical Growth

The numerical increase of the church is measured in membership, baptisms, and attendance levels. When a church functions in the power of God, it gathers a harvest of new believers. God, through the witness of believers, adds numbers to the body of Christ. The evangelistic potential of Sunday School ministry provides the church a key methodology for realizing numerical growth.

What is your perception of your church's Sunday School vision in terms of numerical growth next year and beyond? Do you expect to grow in and through Sunday School ministry? Identify some numerical goals.

ESSENTIALS FOR EXCELLENCE

Spiritual Transformation

The Lord does not intend for kingdom growth to be shallow. Hence, spiritual transformation—God's work of changing a believer into the likeness of Jesus by creating a new identity in Christ and by empowering a lifelong relationship of love, trust, and obedience to glorify God—is critical. Sunday School ministry that relies on the biblical model of instruction that leads to spiritual transformation will prove to be an effective methodology for life-changing growth.

What is your perception of your church's Sunday School vision in terms of spiritual transformation next year and beyond? What could be evidence of spiritual growth in the lives of the people touched by your church through Sunday School ministry?

Ministry Expansion

This result describes the additional doors of ministry the Holy Spirit opens through the lives of believers as a church increases numerically and grows spiritually. Every believer has potential for ministry, and many believers look for the church to provide opportunities for ministry. Sunday School classes and departments become outlets for ministry.

What is your perception of your church's Sunday School vision in terms of ministry expansion next year and beyond? Do classes and departments encourage and provide opportunities for members to minister? Identify one example.

Kingdom Advance

A church is not all it should be if it increases numerically, develops spiritually, and expands its ministry but does not involve itself in missions. Sunday School ministry supports missions through its promotion of missions giving and enlistment of members to participate on mission teams.

What is your perception of your church's Sunday School vision in terms of kingdom advance next year and beyond? How does your Sunday School ministry support missions?

Connecting Sunday School to Life

Your Vision for Your Church's Sunday School Ministry
Now write your vision for your church's Sunday School ministry. What do you see Sunday School ministry becoming or helping the church to accomplish? Focus on the same four result areas.

My Vision for Our Church's Sunday School Ministry

Numerical Growth

Spiritual Transformation

Ministry Expansion

Missions advance

Compare your personal Sunday School vision with your perception of the congregation's vision. List similarities and differences.

Similarities	Differences

Vision and the Leader

Similarities represent points of agreement and areas in which action can be taken and resources and energies focused. If you are convinced the similarities are part of a God-given vision, then take advantage of the opportunity to plan actions that achieve the desired results.

- Identify actions that need to be taken immediately.
- Decide who needs to be included in planning and implementation.
- Determine what resources are needed.
- Develop a time line to do the work and to do evaluation and follow-up.

But what about the differences? Differences challenge the leader. More often than not, leadership is the key to vision achievement. Even people who have a vision need someone to step forward to lead them in fulfilling that vision.

Seldom does a visionary leader lead with 100 percent support. The visionary leader needs to be certain of the vision and know how to deal with conflict in the face of achieving the vision. Look back at the four biblical leaders for some additional truths about visionary leadership.

- These leaders understood the difference between having a vision and being visionary.
- They clearly were ahead of those they led.
- They spent time casting the vision to those who would follow.
- They guided their followers through a time of change.
- They accepted that not everyone supported the changes.
- They were undaunted by some who initially shared the vision but later rejected the leader and his change initiative.
- They continued to provide visionary leadership in the face of conflict.
- They reaffirmed their vision through an ongoing relationship with the Lord God who had instilled the vision.
- They functioned from strength outside of themselves.
- They stayed focused.
- They were committed to excellence.

What other lessons can you learn from these leaders? Before continuing, spend time in prayer.

- Reaffirm your call, including to the specific place where you are leader.
- Reaffirm the vision that is driving what you do.
- Ask God for help in knowing how to lead from that vision.
- Admit your concern about differences, difficulties, and conflicts.
- Commit yourself to the task in spite of opposition.
- Ask for an endowment of His strength and wisdom to lead according to His calling, purpose, and vision.

Evaluating with Vision

On the credenza behind my desk is a photograph from a family vacation. That photo captured a point in time. It shows where we were, what we were doing, and how we looked, including such details as how we were dressed and whether our hair was combed. As I compare my wife and myself with the way we look today, I am surprised by how much difference 24 months can make! One of us (me!) looks a little heavier today than then. One of us (me!) looks a little older today. Perhaps we can't do anything about looking older. As for looking a little heavier today, well, the photograph tells me I need to make a few changes in my lifestyle.

Comparing what was with what is and what is with what is desired is evaluation. Evaluation is like a snapshot; it records something at a point in time. Sometimes we like what we see. At other times we are reminded that some corrections are needed.

We have envisioned what we want to see take place in our church through Sunday School ministry. We are eager to get started, to act to make the vision reality. But first, it is important to spend time assessing the situation.

Actually, while annual evaluation needs to be a major part of preparation for another year of ministry, consider making evaluation part of your ongoing routine as a leader. Ongoing evaluation helps you be constantly aware of whether progress is being made, lapses exist, adjustments or correctives are needed. You learn which plans worked well; which leaders are reliable; where you have succeeded; what your strengths are; and so forth.

If evaluation is only a once-a-year thing, you may miss the joy and encouragement that comes from realizing just how beautifully the work is being done. Most of us are eager to see those vacation pictures as soon as possible. That is one of the benefits of instant and digital cameras.

On the other hand, if we do only annual evaluation, over the longer period of time some of the weaknesses or bad habits may become deeply entangled in the fabric of practice. Changing them may become more difficult.

Making a Personal Connection:
Some Lenses Through Which to View Sunday School Ministry

Evaluation assumes a standard against which effectiveness may be measured. These standards become the lenses through which ongoing evaluation, future planning, and plan implementation are to be viewed. As with vacation photos, different lenses give a different perspective on the same subject.

The Kingdom Perspective

Jesus had a kingdom vision. He came announcing the coming of the kingdom (Mark 1:15); told stories about the kingdom (Matt. 13); and taught His followers to pray for the kingdom (Luke 11:2). Indeed, the focus of His life, death, and resurrection was the kingdom.

Following Jesus' model, then, the first lens through which we look during evaluation is a kingdom perspective. Don't confuse institutions and organizations with the kingdom of God. Are efforts focused on building a great church or Sunday School; or are leaders and members first and foremost trying to be kingdom people doing kingdom work to the honor and glory of the King?

Look through the kingdom lens. What do you see in your church and Sunday School ministry to give evidence that the focus truly is on the kingdom of God and not the kingdom of self, institutional success, or denominational recognition?

<u>**The Kingdom Lens**</u>

The Great Commission

The Great Commission (Matt. 28:18-20) is to be the driving force behind every New Testament church. The mission mandate is to "make disciples." Doing so includes going on mission to declare the good news, assimilating believers into the life of the church and discipling them as ministry multipliers, and teaching them obedience to the instructions of Christ.

Look through the lens of the Great Commission. As you view your church and Sunday School ministry through this lens, can you identify some ways to illustrate that the Great Commission is the driving force behind your church's ministry plans and actions?

<u>**The Great Commission Lens**</u>

Connecting Sunday School to Life

The Functions of a Church

Acts 2:42-47 describe the actions of the church in Jerusalem following the empowering of the Spirit on the Day of Pentecost. We have come to identify these actions as essential functions for any church that would be fashioned according to the New Testament model: evangelism (vv. 38,41), discipleship (v. 42), fellowship (vv. 42,44,46), ministry (v. 45), and worship (vv. 42,46-47).

Now view your church and Sunday School ministry through the lens of church functions. Identify at least one way each function is part of your church practice. Does your church ministry plan demonstrate balance in carrying out these functions? How does Sunday School ministry support each one?

<u>**Church Functions Lens**</u>

Community Context and Culture

Your church is part of some community. It may be located downtown, in the suburbs, in a neighborhood, or in the country. That community may be populated by one predominant race, age group, or economic class. Whatever the situation, your church likely reflects some aspects of the community if the people who attend actually live in the community where the church is located.

A church also has a culture. In this sense culture is the local context of church life that influences a church's perception of itself and leads to its unique identity and style as a church. Every church develops a culture whether the church has a long history or is a new start. The church's culture influences "the way we do church." It can be a powerful force that attracts people or a serious barrier that neutralizes its sphere of influence. Factors that are part of a church's culture include the mix of generational perspectives, age of members, race and ethnicity, gender issues, household status, lifestyle affinity, educational levels, local church history, community and community influences, and more.

View your church through its cultural lens. Learn about the people in the community and their needs, interests, and hurts. Capture a snapshot of the community geographically, demographically, culturally, and spiritually.

<u>**A Snapshot of Our Community**</u>

Geo-demographic information usually can be obtained from the United States Census Bureau, county and city planning departments, newspaper offices, local chambers of commerce, and builders/realtors/utility companies. Strategic and growth planning assistance is available through some state Baptist conventions and the North American Mission Board.

Sunday School Definition and Purpose

This resource is concerned primarily with Sunday School ministry and how it is pivotal to helping a church fulfill its vision. Therefore we would do well to define what we mean by Sunday School: *Sunday School is the foundational strategy in a local church for leading people to faith in the Lord Jesus Christ and for building on-mission Christians through open Bible study groups that engage people in evangelism, discipleship, fellowship, ministry, and worship.*

Some key concepts in this definition will be explained more completely in subsequent sections of this book. For now simply think of Sunday School as a basic framework for leading people to Christ (evangelism) and starting them on the journey of a meaningful relationship with Him (discipleship). This work is accomplished through open Bible study groups—Sunday School classes and departments. An open group or open Sunday School class is an intentionally evangelistic group that gathers around a study of God's Word. It serves as a primary entry point into the church for unbelievers.

Look at your church and its Sunday School ministry through this lens.
- *Is your Sunday School functioning as a program organization focused on teaching as an end in itself, or does it provide a basic framework for your church's efforts in evangelism and discipleship through Bible teaching?*
- *Is your Sunday School built around open Bible study group concepts?*

Sunday School Definition and Purpose

Ten Best Practices of Effective Sunday School Ministry

The best practices represent essential actions for planning and implementing an effective Sunday School ministry. When used as a lens for evaluation, they can help you see how well you are doing what needs to be done. You will find these actions explained further in Section 2 and detailed on the **CD-ROM** and in *Ten Best Practices to Make Your Sunday School Work.*

Connecting Sunday School to Life

1. *Commit to the strategy.* We commit to Sunday School as the foundational strategy in our church for doing the work of the Great Commission.
2. *Organize with purpose.* We organize our Sunday School ministry to accomplish the objectives of leading people to faith in the Lord Jesus Christ and building on-mission Christians.
3. *Build kingdom leaders.* We build leaders who demonstrate a commitment to the kingdom, Christ as Lord, the ministry to which they have been called, the church, and the mission mandate Christ has given.
4. *Develop soul-winners.* We lead all leaders and members to become soul-winners and witnesses for Christ in all life settings, including the home.
5. *Win the lost.* We engage in evangelistic actions that result in winning the lost to Christ as well as in other actions that focus on the unchurched and reclaim the spiritually indifferent.
6. *Assimilate people.* We assimilate individuals and families into the life of the church and facilitate their growth as disciples of Christ.
7. *Partner with families.* We partner with parents and families to build the home as the center of biblical guidance.
8. *Teach to transform.* We engage individuals and families in the biblical model of instruction that leads to spiritual transformation.
9. *Mobilize for ministry.* We take deliberate actions to mobilize people to meet with compassion the needs of individuals and families.
10. *Multiply leaders and units.* We develop and implement an intentional process for continually multiplying leaders and new Bible study groups.

Using this lens, take a wide-angle view of your Sunday School ministry. Are all the pieces in the picture? Do you see areas of need? What are you doing well? Where do you need to refocus?

Ten Best Practices Lens

• Things we are doing well

• Areas of need

• Areas in which we need to refocus our attention

ESSENTIALS FOR EXCELLENCE

Instruments for Doing Evaluation

If the standards noted in the previous section are the lenses for looking at how well you are doing, then the instruments in this section are like the cameras that take the photographs. Each gives a different view and reveals a new perspective. Put the results together and you should have an overall picture of your church's Sunday School ministry.

Church and Community Assessment

The data gathered as you viewed your church and community through the cultural lens will enable you to do a church and community comparative assessment. This information can be studied and compared with church data collected through church record-keeping practices, informal surveys of the community and church membership, and data on the Annual Church Profile (ACP).

1. How many people live in the community and fall under the church's influence?
2. What are the characteristics of the people in terms of age, family structure, education, profession, religion, and so forth?
3. What are their values, interests, hurts, fears?
4. What do they already know about the gospel?
5. How does the makeup of your church membership compare to the makeup of the community population?
- What was the population 10 years ago? Five years ago?
- What are population projections?
- Has the growth of the church kept pace with the growth rate of the community?
6. Compare the total resident church membership or Sunday School enrollment with attendance over the past three years. What percentage of the membership/enrollment attend worship services and Bible study?
- Compare the enrollment and average participation of each age group in Bible study for the past three years.
- Are significant increases or decreases evident in any age group?
- What implications do these changes have on future ministry directions?
7. Compare the age-group percentages represented in the church with the age-group percentages of the community population.
- Are there major differences?
- What actions need to be taken to bring the age-group percentages in line with one another?

Connecting Sunday School to Life

Take a good look at the snapshot of your community. Now examine the snapshot of your church. How much alike or different are they?
Comparing Church and Community Makeup

Last Year's Strategic Annual Plan

Review last year's annual plan for general needs, priority needs, objectives, goals, assignments, completion dates, and other pertinent details that were agreed upon or adopted. They can give you a picture of how well you did in light of what you planned to do. Ask these questions:

- Did the needs identified in last year's plan prove to be legitimate? Was the prioritization of those needs accurate? What new needs and priorities surfaced during the year? Were they merged into the plan? How?
- Were objectives achieved? Goals attained? Did achieving the objectives and attaining the goals move the church toward fulfillment of its vision?
- Were action plans focused enough to contribute to goal attainment?
- Did the individuals who had assignments actually fulfill their responsibilities? How could greater support have been given to them?
- Was the work completed in a timely fashion?

Take a snapshot using last year's strategic annual plan. What do you see? Did you do what you planned to do?
Last Year's Strategic Annual Plan

Sunday School Ministry and General Church Records
The weekly records we keep for Sunday School should do more than just tell us how many we had on a given Sunday. They give us a picture of how we are doing in several areas. By comparing current data with records from previous years, we can see patterns or trends. Here are some statistical areas to examine:

- Attendance
- Enrollment
- New Members
- Losses
- Baptisms
- Other Church Additions
- Potential Members
- New Classes/Departments Started
- Leaders Trained
- Other

Ready. Say "cheese." (Snapshot) Based on this data, what do you see? This is an important picture of your church. If you don't see numbers of people involved, that can be a warning sign that something is wrong.
<u>Information from Records</u>

Sunday School Growth and Evaluation Plan
This instrument calls attention to key factors that influence the effectiveness of Sunday School ministry. A Sunday School Growth Evaluation Plan Summary Sheet serves as a vital planning tool. See the **CD-ROM** for this form.

Connecting Sunday School to Life

Enrollment

Open enrollment means to enroll people in an open Bible study group anywhere at any time as long as they agree. Follow-up needs to be immediate.

    Current Enrollment: _____

    Recommended Goal: Show an increase from year to year.

Prospects

A prospect is anyone not enrolled in Bible study for whom you have a name and address. Reaching prospects begins with determining whether the person is spiritually lost. If so, evangelistic effort becomes primary.

    Current Number of Prospects: _____

    Recommended Goal: 1:1, or cultivate one spiritually lost person
        for every member already on roll.

Classes or Units

A Bible study class or unit reaches its maximum size in 12-18 months. After that time it tends to be less receptive to new people. New units help keep growth alive.

    Current Class to Enrollment Ratio: _____

    Recommended Goal: 1:20, or one class for every 20 people enrolled.
        Specific age-group ratios need to be considered.

Leaders

A leader is anyone who leads the teaching, reaching, or ministry to members and prospects in a class or department.

    Current Leader-to-Member Ratio: _____

    Recommended Goal: 1:5, or one leader for every five members.

Space

Every church has three types of space: *worship, parking, educational.* If any one of these spaces is at 80 percent capacity, then consider the space full. When preschool space is full, church growth will plateau. Meeting space is needed for each Bible study group. Some groups may meet off site.

    Current Space to Group Ratio: _____

    Recommended Goal: 1:1, or one space for each group

Ministry Contacts

The Sunday School roll is also a list of weekly ministry opportunities. A class needs to be organized for this to happen.

> Current Ministry Contact to Member Ratio: ____
> Recommended Goal: 1:1, or one contact each week for every member

Leaders in Training

Every leader needs to participate in at least one leadership training event annually.

> Current Participation Percentage: ____
> Recommended Participation Goal: 100%

Sunday School Leadership Meetings

Leadership meetings prepare leaders to meet the needs of the people who are the focus of a class or department.

> Current Participation Percentage: ____
> Recommended Goal: At least 75%

Sunday School Attendance

Several factors affect attendance:

- Enrollment: Attendance tends to average between 40 and 60 percent of enrollment. Increase enrollment, and the average attendance potential increases.
- Weekly contacts: Attendance will increase based on an increase in number and types of contacts made.
- Ratio of leaders to members: Attendance is impacted by increasing the number of leaders and decreasing the ratio of leaders to members.
- Number of groups: Attendance is increased by starting and strengthening new Bible study groups that target unreached persons.

> Current Average Attendance to Enrollment Percentage: ____
> Recommended Percentage Goal: 40-60% of enrollment

Participation in Discipleship Ministry

Discipleship groups are designed primarily for believers. They focus on applying God's Word and building on-mission Christians.

> Current Percent of Sunday School Enrollment in Discipleship: ____%
> Recommended Goal: 50%

Connecting Sunday School to Life

Worship

The ratio of Sunday School attendance to worship reflects the effectiveness of assimilation done by the Sunday School. The higher the ratio of Sunday School attendance to worship, the more effective the assimilation and the greater the opportunities for evangelism, discipleship, fellowship, and ministry.

 Current Status _____

 Recommended Goal: Sunday School average attendance at least
  90% of average worship attendance.

Offerings

The projected Sunday School attendance multiplied by the per capita giving number projects total offering potential.

 Current Per Capita Giving and Average Sunday School Attendance: _____

 Recommended Goal: Sunday School attendance multiplied by
  per capita giving number.

FAITH Teams

The number of FAITH Teams in Sunday School should be equal to the number of Bible study groups.

 Current Ratio of FAITH Teams to Sunday School Groups: _____

 Recommended Goal: 1:1, or one team for every group.

Baptisms

One-half of the net enrollment gain usually will be spiritually lost persons; half of that number will be baptized and assimilated into the church in one year.

 Current Ratio: ___

 Recommended Goal: _____

*This instrument captures some important details that other instruments do not. Complete the summary sheet on the **CD-ROM**. Examine the snapshot it provides closely. What areas need priority attention?*

Sunday School Strategy Growth Worksheet (CD-ROM)
Complete the worksheet to get a picture of the potential of your Sunday School ministry and the number of units (classes, departments) and leaders needed to reach that potential. What is your current standing? Where do you need to focus attention in terms of new units and more leaders?

The worksheet on page 33 or the electronic version on the CD-ROM may be used as is. It highlights three critical areas: enrollment, classes/units, leaders. Depending on the size of your Sunday School ministry and the number of units in each age group, you may want to develop a worksheet for each age group. Use this Youth Sunday School example to fill out the form.

Column 1	Insert current total enrollment of all youth classes/departments; let's say you have 25 youth.
Column 2	Insert total number of prospects; for example, 50 youth prospects.
Column 3	Add columns 1 and 2 for total possible enrollment: 75.
Column 4	Insert your enrollment goal for the year. This number may be the same or less than the number in Column 3, depending on your projection of prospects reached. In our example, we project we will reach 35 of our youth prospects. Our enrollment goal would be 60 (25 currently enrolled; 35 prospects reached out of 50).
Column 5	This number represents the maximum number to be enrolled in a youth class and department—not necessarily the desired number, but a maximum. Remember a room is perceived as full when it reaches 80 percent of capacity. A class or department with fewer than 12 or 60, respectively, is in a position to grow. Classes that are at the maximum are less likely to grow. A new unit is needed.
Column 6	Insert number of classes currently provided for the age group (For our example, 3).
Column 7	To determine the number of classes needed, divide the enrollment goal (Column 4) by the maximum number class enrollment (for youth, 12). (In our example, 60/12 = 5).
Column 8	To determine the number of new classes needed, subtract Column 6 from Column 7 (In our example, 5-3 = 2).
Column 9	This column is the maximum ratio of leaders to pupils. For youth, one leader for every 12 youth learners in a class.
Column 10	Insert number of leaders currently working with youth in Sunday School (For our example, 3).
Column 11	To determine total number of leaders needed based on potential enrollment, divide Column 4 by Column 9 (in our example, 60/12 = 5).
Column 12	To determine the number of new leaders needed, subtract Column 10 from Column 11 (In our example, 5-3 = 2).

$$1200$$
$$.8$$
$$\overline{960.0}$$

Connecting Sunday School to Life

Sunday School Strategy Growth Worksheet ☆

Age Group	ENROLLMENT				CLASSES				LEADERS			
	1	2	3	4	5	6	7	8	9	10	11	12
	Present Enrollment	Prospects	Total Possible Enrollment (1+2=)	Enrollment Goal	Suggested Maximum Enrollment/Class	No. Classes Currently	Total No. Classes Needed (4/5=)	No. *New* Classes Needed (7-6=)	Maximum Ratio Leaders: Pupils	No. Leaders Currently	Total Leaders Needed (4/9=)	No. *New* Leaders Needed (11-10=)
PRESCHOOL												
Babies					12				1:2			
Ones–Twos					12				1:3			
Threes–Pre-K					16				1:4			
Kindergarten					20				1:5			
CHILDREN Ages 6-11 years / Grades 1-6					24				1:6			
YOUTH Ages 12-17 years / Grades 7-12					12/ Class 60/ Dept.				1:12			
COLLEGIATE/ YOUNG ADULT Ages 18-24 years					40/ Class 160/ Dept.				1:40 (teacher) 1:4 (all leaders)			
ADULT Ages 25 years-up					40/ Class 160/ Dept.				1:40 (teacher) 1:4 (all leaders)			
SPECIAL EDUCATION Low-functioning (severely disabled)					6				1:1			
High-functioning (readers)					15				1:4			
In between					12				1:2– 1:3			

Space Analysis

A church needs to provide the best possible space for each Bible study group. Use the guidelines provided in the Meeting Space Specifications Chart (also on the **CD-ROM**) to analyze the space you have available.

This snapshot of your physical facilities will help you identify the total number of spaces available and the dimensions of each. It also will help you evaluate if the space is being used to its maximum potential.

Meeting Space Specifications Chart

Age Group	Space/Person	Maximum Attendance	Room Size	Leader: Learner Ratio
Preschool				
Babies	35 sq. ft.	12	420 sq. ft.	1:2
Ones–Twos	35 sq. ft.	12	420 sq. ft.	1:3
Threes–Pre-K	35 sq. ft.	16	560 sq. ft.	1:4
Kindergarten	35 sq. ft.	20	700 sq. ft.	1:5
Children				
Grades 1-6	20-25 sq. ft.	24	480-600 sq. ft.	1:6
Youth				
Gr. 7-12 (class)	10-12 sq. ft.	12	120-144 sq. ft.	1:12
Gr. 7-12 (dept.)	8-10 sq. ft.	60	480-600 sq. ft.	1:12
Young Adults 18-24 yrs				
Department	10 sq. ft.			
Class	12-15 sq. ft.	20-25	240-375 sq. ft.	1:4
Dual Use	15-18 sq. ft.	20-25	300-450 sq. ft.	
Adults 25 yrs-up				
Department	10 sq. ft.			
Class	12-15 sq. ft.	20-25	240-375 sq. ft.	1:4
Dual Use	15-18 sq. ft.	20-25	300-450 sq. ft.	
Special Education				
Low-functioning	25 sq. ft.	1:1	480 sq. ft. (10 sq. ft. per person for wheelchairs)	
High-functioning		1:4		
In between		1:2-1:3		

Equipment and Furnishings Analysis

The teaching-learning climate is affected by the equipment and furnishings that are available. Different age groups need different kinds of equipment and furnishings appropriate to the physical size of those using the space and the teaching approaches used with them. The following lists, and on the **CD-ROM** (especially age-group e-books), indicate recommended items for each age group.

Review the equipment and furnishings list. Walk through your facility to overview what equipment and furnishings currently are available. As you view this picture, consider the kind of impression your space, equipment, and furnishings leave on those individuals and families your church is trying to reach. Is it an attractive picture? What can be done to make it better?

Recommended Equipment and Furnishings List

Symbols: **x** - recommended
            o - optional
            all - specialized equipment purchased in limited quantity for use by all ages.

Preschool General Items (see CD-ROM, Preschool, E-Book Additional Resources)

General	B	1	2	3	4	K	All	B-2	3-K	B-K
Rest mats or towels		x	o					x		o
Cribs (hospital 27"x42")	x	o						x		x
Adult rocking chair (2)	x							x		x
Solid surface floor mat (42" x 42")	x									
Wall cabinet (50" above floor)	x	x	x	x	x	x		x	x	x
Trash receptacles with lid	x	x	x	x	x	x		x	x	x
Diaper bag cubbies or hooks	x	x	x							
Vinyl changing pad		x	x							
Open shelf/closed back for toys (26"x36"x12")		o						o		o
Child safety gate										o
Water source for disinfecting	x	x	x					x		x
Slow cookers	x							x		x
Folding screen for nursing area	x							x		x
Rocking boat with enclosed steps		o								
Small counter top refrigerator	o									

Recommended Equipment and Furnishings List, cont'd.

Children's, Youth, Adult, and Special Education Departments/Classes

Equipment	Children	Youth	Adults	Special Education[10]
Chairs (age appropriate)	x[1]	x[2]	x[2]	x[2]
Coat rack	x	x	x	x
Resources cabinet	x	x		x
Tables	x[3]	x[5]	o	x (4-6 members)
Shelves	x[6]	x	x	o
Book racks	x[7]	x	o	o
Tackboard or bulletin boards	x[8]	x	x	x
Wastebasket	x	x	x	x
Podium/table for teacher	o	o		o
Sink	o			o
Autoharp	x			o
Cassette player	x	x	x	o
TV/VCR combination	o	o	o	o
CD player	o	x	o	x
Piano	o	o	o	o
Chalk/marker board(s)	x	x[4]	x[4]	x[4]
Tear sheets	x	x	x	x

Equipment	Children	Youth	Adults	
Felt-tip markers	x	x	x	x
Other art/writing supplies	x	x	x	x
Picture rails	x[9]			

[1]Recommended chair sizes for children:
  Grades 1&2: 12-13 inches
  Grades 3&4: 14-15 inches
  Grades 5&6: 16-17 inches
[2]Standard chairs 18 inches above the floor.
[3]Tabletops for children should be 10 inches above chair seats.
[4]36x45 inches min. for hanging boards; freestanding and movable boards of comparable size or larger are preferred.
[5]Folding chairs for youth should be no more than 28 inches high.
[6]14-19 inches deep, 42-46 inches high, and 3-4 feet long with shelves 12-14 inches apart.
[7]Bookracks should be 42-46 inches high and 30-42 inches long.
[8]Tackboards should be 24-30 inches in height and 6-10 feet in length with the bottom edge 24-30 inches above the floor.
[9]Picture rails should be about 30 inches above the floor on the front wall & 12 feet long.
[10]Wheelchairs: class doors should be 32 inches wide; hallways, 48 inches wide; wheelchairs should fit underneath tables; accessible rest room nearby may dictate classroom location.

Connecting Sunday School to Life

A Look at the Big Picture (CD-ROM Evaluation Worksheets)

These evaluation instruments provide a collection of pictures of your church and its Sunday School ministry. Put them all together, and you get the big picture or at least a collage that allows you to see several things at once.

1. Is your church functioning from a kingdom perspective? Are leaders kingdom people doing kingdom work for the glory of the King? What do you see that makes you believe this is true?

2. Is your church driven by the Great Commission? What do you see in your church picture as evidence?

3. Are the five functions of a New Testament church a balanced part of your church's ministry practice? Is Sunday School ministry an important element for helping your church carrying out those functions? Why?

4. How is your church using Sunday School? As one program among many, or as a basic plan for carrying out the Great Commission assignment? Do others share your understanding? If not, what needs to be done to cast the vision of the potential of Sunday School ministry?

5. How did you assess your Sunday School ministry in terms of the ten best practices (essential actions)? What can you affirm? What needs surfaced?

6. How do you see your church's efforts in light of last year's strategic plan?

7. Develop a statistical chart or graph to show gains or losses in the categories listed on page 28. Based on those statistics, is your church growing (an increase of 10 percent or more), plateaued, or declining?

8. Continue to study the Sunday School Growth and Evaluation Plan and the summary chart. What do they reveal that other leaders need to see?

9. Review the Sunday School Strategy Growth Worksheet.
   - Do you currently have enough units to care for those enrolled in your church's Sunday School ministry? Enough leaders for the number of teaching-ministry units in your organizational structure?
   - How many new units need to be started to care for your people potential? How many new leaders are needed to care for this potential?

10. What does the picture of your physical space reveal?
    - How many total meeting spaces do you have available? How many organizational units do you currently have? How many new organizational units do you project?
    - How much new meeting space is needed? What options do you have?

11. According to your furnishings and equipment snapshot, what items are needed this year?
    - Make a list; determine priorities.
    - Develop a plan for securing what is needed through the church's budget and purchasing processes.
    - What did you find that needs to be removed because it is inappropriate, unsafe, or not functional?

Communicating the Vision

Look back at our biblical examples of visionary leaders.
*   With whom did they share their vision?
*   Why did each think it was important to share the vision?
*   How did they share their vision?
*   What evidence exists that they were successful in sharing their vision?

Some leaders are so eager to launch into action that they fail to spend sufficient time sharing the vision, preparing other leaders for action, and equipping them for the work to be done. Leaders who move too quickly run the risk of alienating their followers or at least of running off and leaving them behind. A visionary leader cannot achieve a vision by himself. If he is truly a leader, he won't even try. He will engage others.

As you think about the vision you have for your church and specifically its Sunday School ministry, how can you share what you see? How can you help others see the vision? What do you want them to understand about the vision?

Communicating the Vision of Being a Kingdom-Focused Church

The existence and activity of the church is rooted in God's purposes to bring His kingdom to fulfillment. The kingdom is present wherever the will and reign of God are established in people's lives through the presence of Jesus Christ.

Perhaps then, what many pastors and church leaders need is not so much a new focus as a refocus on being a kingdom people on a kingdom mission doing kingdom work under the authority of the King. The focus is on the church's purpose, not its programs; its functions, not the forms; the message, not the methods; the God-given results, not human aspirations. The outcome when God's people faithfully obey His will and His Word in the world will be kingdom growth—God's supernatural work through His people to accomplish His kingdom's purposes.

Through The Kingdom-Focused Church Model and Process

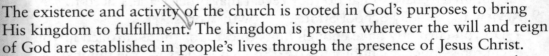

If the focus is to be on the kingdom, then what does a kingdom-focused church look like? What does it do? The Kingdom-Focused Church Model and Process (MAP) can help us see what a kingdom-focused church is and how it works. (For more details, see *The Kingdom-Focused Church* by Gene Mims.)

Connecting Sunday School to Life

- *A biblically-based, comprehensive view or model of church* both in terms of what it is and what it does in relationship to bringing a spiritually lost person into the kingdom. It identifies biblical principles—purpose and functions; describes effective church practice—strategies and methodologies; and points to kingdom results—corporate and personal, that come through the supernatural activity of God.

  Results which

- *A process* for leading people through stages of spiritual transformation and leading a church toward realizing God-given results. It shows the working relationship of the various elements in the process.

- *An evaluative, diagnostic tool* for helping churches assess their ministries and practices in light of biblical principles and desired results. It is here that the Kingdom-Focused Church Model and Process offers greatest potential. Through dialogue, leaders can consider answers to these probing questions: (1) What do you think God wants to see happening in your church? (2) What does the Bible say a church should be doing? (3) What prevents your church from doing what it should and realizing the blessing God wants to provide? (4) What is needed to overcome these hindrances?

  Deacons   Bonnie?

Pervading the entire Kingdom-Focused Church Model and Process are four fundamental truths.

*Deacon
Pastor Bonnie?*

- *The lordship of Christ* (Matt. 28:18; Rom 10:9-10; Phil. 2:5-11)—Jesus is Lord of the kingdom and Lord of the church. He is the authority. Those who believe in Him—citizens of the kingdom—are His servants. Faithful servants respond with obedience to the commands of their masters. Jesus issued a mandate: make disciples. Therefore, His faithful followers will not hesitate to obey, for He is Lord.

- *The Holy Spirit* (Acts 1:8)—Without the Spirit, the church is powerless. Lost persons cannot be saved, believers cannot grow, and the church cannot be guided without the Holy Spirit's indwelling presence. We must yield ourselves to Him before we make decisions.

- *Corporate prayer* (Acts 4:25-31)—Prayer opens the church to God's will and direction. Corporate prayer is the church in relationship with the Father, hearing from Him, and discerning His will and purpose.

- *Church leadership* (Eph. 4:11-12)—Effective leadership is critical to church life and ministry. Church leaders—the primary one being the pastor—are to (1) lead the church to accomplish the Great Commission, and (2) bring every believer for whom the leader is accountable to maturity in Christ. Leaders are called by God to follow Christ in a life of discipleship, using their spiritual gifts productively in the economy of God.

  Deacons

ESSENTIALS FOR EXCELLENCE

Elements of the Kingdom-Focused Church Model and Process
The Kingdom-Focused Church Model and Process dialogue is centered on a review of biblical principles, church practice, and kingdom results.

Biblical Principles
Biblical principles are the primary teachings from the Scriptures that direct the scope and work of the church in relationship to its efforts to lead an unbeliever from spiritual lostness to faithful service as an obedient disciple of Christ. You used these principles as you took snapshots of your church.

• The Great Commission (Matt. 28:18-20) is the driving force of missions and evangelism for believers and churches in every generation. To achieve its mandate to make disciples—the Lord challenges His followers to engage in three actions—go, baptize, and teach—that become the basis for intentional church practice. Without the driving force of the Great Commission, church practice will be little more than a misguided attempt to gain numbers, increase enrollments, discover methods, or use new techniques.

• Church functions (Acts 2:38-47) are the biblical actions a church takes to fulfill its purpose for being (Matt. 28:16-20). Correlating with the mission mandate of the Great Commission, these five functions are the gateway to effectiveness in the contemporary church.

Evangelism (Acts 2:38-41) is the process of sharing the gospel with lost persons and winning people to Christ, which brings them into the kingdom of God. The purpose for going, the announcement of the good news is the critical first step in making disciples. *Discipleship* (Acts 2:42-43) is a lifelong journey of obedience to Christ that transforms a person's values and behavior and results in ministry in one's home, church, and world. Discipleship is the process of carrying out the admonition to teach obedience to the commands of Christ. *Fellowship* (Acts 2:42,46-47) is the intimate spiritual relationship that Christians share with God and other believers through their relationship with Jesus Christ. Fellowship is a result of being assimilated into the body, which is symbolized by the act of baptism in the name of the Triune God.

Ministry (Acts 2:44-45) is meeting another person's need in Jesus' name, expressed as service to persons inside the church and as missions to persons outside the church. Ministry naturally follows evangelism and discipleship in the Christian developmental process, though all occur simultaneously. *Worship* (Acts 2:46-47) is the response of a person to the presence, holiness, and revelation of Almighty God. Worship includes recognizing the Lord's authority, acknowledging His worthiness, and obeying His Commission.

Church Practice and Kingdom Results
The phrase *Church Practice* describes the essential actions, intentionally balanced strategies, and specific methodologies a church uses to achieve its

Connecting Sunday School to Life

purpose and to engage people in evangelism, discipleship, fellowship, ministry, and worship. Examining church practice requires a church to wrestle with the questions What do we intend to be? Where do we want to go? What is the most effective way to do our work to make the greatest difference in people's lives? Through its strategies and methodologies, effective church practice addresses three stages of spiritual transformation in the life of a believer.

1. *Making disciples* represents the efforts of a church to win the spiritually lost and begin the assimilation of new believers into the body of Christ.

2. *Maturing believers* represents the efforts of a church in discipleship as it intensifies the teaching and continues the assimilation of new believers and members.

3. *Multiplying ministries* represents the efforts of a church to provide members opportunities for service and missions.

Church strategies refers to the clear and deliberate intentions and plans of action that are necessary if a church is to achieve its objective in its distinctive environment. Four key strategies are identified:

1. A *corporate worship strategy* exists to celebrate God's grace and mercy, to proclaim God's truth, and to evangelize the lost. This occurs in an atmosphere of encountering the presence, holiness, and revelation of Almighty God. As an open gathering of believers and unbelievers, corporate worship becomes an entry point for unbelievers into the church.

2. An *open group strategy* exists to lead people to faith in the Lord Jesus Christ and to build on-mission Christians by engaging people in foundational evangelism, discipleship, fellowship, ministry, and worship through ongoing and short-term evangelistic Bible study units. These Bible study groups include believers and unbelievers together in an atmosphere of compassion. The effectiveness of the strategy will be realized as existing Bible study groups birth new groups and develop new leaders.

3. A *closed group strategy* exists to build kingdom leaders and to equip believers to serve by engaging people in discipleship that moves them toward spiritual transformation. This takes place primarily through short-term, self-contained training units in an atmosphere of accountability to God and others.

4. A *ministry team strategy* exists to build up the body of Christ to accomplish the work of service within the church (Acts 6:1-3) and to be involved in missions outside the church through new or existing kingdom units (Acts 13:1-3).

Methodologies are the means for carrying out a strategy, and translate into forms, structures, work, leadership, participants, and resources. For example, Sunday School is a methodology for carrying out the open-group strategy.

Kingdom results are the supernatural activity of God expressed through the body of Christ and reflected in the changed lives of His people. Earlier we looked at four kinds of results that occur when a body of believers obeys

faithfully and with kingdom focus: numerical growth, spiritual transformation, ministry expansion, and kingdom advance.

Communicating a Vision of Sunday School Carrying Out the Functions of a Church

Sunday School and Evangelism

Your Sunday School ministry should focus on obedience to Christ in the work of evangelism. Teachers, leaders, and members should constantly be reaching people for Bible study. They must be dedicated to seeking, discovering, and inviting spiritually lost people to participate in open Bible study groups.

Evangelism is the heart of Sunday School ministry. It is Bible study that is comprised of an intentional mix of believers and unbelievers in an atmosphere of compassion to share the gospel. The key word is *intentional*. For most people, inviting lost work associates, that neighbor two houses down from yours, and parents of your child's friend does not come naturally. We must intentionally move outside our comfort zones.

One great threat to the effectiveness of your Sunday School is the tendency of a class or department to become a crystallized group that focuses on the needs and interests of current members to the exclusion of those who do not yet know Christ or the fellowship of His people. Crystallized classes or groups may become so focused on "deeper Bible study" that they often unintentionally exclude those who are new to the study of God's Word. Or a class can so enjoy its own fellowship that "outsiders" who need to be reached are excluded.

Sunday School as an open-group strategy is marked by evangelistic Bible teaching through ongoing Bible study classes and other Bible study groups that are always open for anyone. This means providing foundational Bible study for preschoolers and younger children from which they will be encouraged to respond positively to the message of salvation as soon as they are able to do so. It means providing an atmosphere in older children's, student, and adult Bible study groups that encourages unsaved people to come to faith in Christ and encourages believers to lead others to Christ. It means seizing every opportunity the Holy Spirit provides to present the gospel through Bible teaching.

Sunday School provides a natural churchwide evangelism training network to equip members to share their faith with unbelievers. The age-graded Sunday School ministry provides the best organizational structure for organizing your church's evangelistic, outreach, and ministry visitation effort. The FAITH Sunday School Evangelism Strategy® is a process for doing this work. (See the FAITH e-book on the **CD-ROM**.)

Starting new Sunday School classes, departments, and other Bible study groups is a priority for those who see Sunday School as an open-group strategy.

Connecting Sunday School to Life

New units consistently seek, discover, and involve more lost people than do existing classes or departments.

Each new Sunday School unit has the potential to reach 10 unsaved people for Christ. Special events such as Vacation Bible School, January Bible Study, and other short-term Bible study groups also support the evangelistic work of your church.

Sunday School and Discipleship

Discipleship is a process that begins after conversion and continues throughout a believer's life. Evangelism begins this process, fellowship contributes to it, and ministry grows out of it. Discipleship is not an option for Christians.

Sunday School can provide foundational discipleship that places people in Bible study groups where they can grow in their understanding of God's Word and obedience to His commands. Although you want the members of your class to grow in their understanding of the Bible, knowledge alone should not be the end result. Neither is it enough to understand a biblical truth and apply it to an area of your life. Your teaching should facilitate the work of the Holy Spirit in spiritually transforming the lives of your learners. (See Section 3.)

Sunday School alone cannot provide all that believers need in their spiritual growth. Genuine discipleship involves leading people to incorporate biblical truth in the total fabric of their hearts, minds, will, and actions. Participation in your church's Discipleship ministry will greatly enhance your members' spiritual growth. Involvement in other areas of your church's ministries—missions and music, for example—helps your people grow in Christlikeness.

I once taught a class of adults in their 30s and 40s. One Sunday, several members with kids ages 13-15 were lamenting that their precious children of years past had turned into strange creatures called teenagers. These parents shared stories—some funny, some not so—about the challenges they faced.

The next week I came across a brochure promoting *The Five Love Languages of Teenagers* by Gary Chapman. The ad read "Learn how to speak and understand the same 'love language' of your child, teen, or spouse."

The following Sunday I couldn't wait to get to class. "Is this something that might help some of you?" Before I finished reading the course description, someone had started a signup sheet to enroll in the course. You can imagine the pastor's response when I ask if our church could offer this discipleship course. "We already have eight people who want to attend" I said, "and one of our members will serve as facilitator." Word spread to other members who had teenagers. The course was full before the resource was ever purchased!

As a Sunday School leader, no one should know better the spiritual needs of your members. Let your pastor or other church leader know what those needs are so your church can focus on specific topics or issues.

Sunday School and Fellowship

Sunday School places people in groups and calls for Bible teaching that facilitates the building of relationships in a ministry environment of grace, acceptance, support, and encouragement. Small groups provide opportunities for participants to interact with God's Word, the teacher, and one another.

Sunday School is made up of classes, departments, and other Bible study groups that provide additional opportunities for people to build fellowship beyond the time the group gathers for Bible study. Some of these gatherings may be social functions that allow members to become better acquainted and to invite their unchurched and unsaved friends. Individuals who are serving in leadership positions in other areas of Sunday School should always be included in the fellowship activities for their age group.

One of the most effective efforts at building fellowship are those times when members pray or work together. As a FAITH Team Leader, I experience one of my greatest joys as I work closely with two other members of my class each semester. A close bond develops as we review homework, pray together, encourage one another, travel to the homes of those we visit, minister to members and prospects, and rejoice with those who pray to receive Christ. I am a better teacher because of the fellowship that happens outside the Sunday morning session.

Sunday School and Ministry

Through the Holy Spirit, God gives Christians spiritual gifts and empowers them to use those gifts in His service. Paul made clear that these gifts were given "to produce what is beneficial" (1 Cor. 12:7). Every member of your Sunday School who professes Christ has a spiritual gift. Help your people discover their gifts and then identify opportunities for members to become involved in ongoing actions of ministry. Direct assignments to members, such as to adult care group leaders. Involve them in specific ministry actions in one-on-one or family-to-family ministry situations. It is important that you as a leader make your members aware of ministry needs both within and outside the church.

The needs of specific groups offer unique opportunities. For example, new parents can benefit significantly from acts of service that help them establish relationships with a church. At one time three members of my Adult Sunday School coed class were expecting children. (Have you ever tried adjusting the heating/cooling thermostat when three women are in varying stages of pregnancy?) Although our class was organized into care teams, several members wanted to establish a more specific group to minister to these families.

These members called themselves The Stork Team! This team began its ministry in earnest when the expectant mother was two months from delivery. One team member met with the family to discuss any dietary restrictions and,

Connecting Sunday School to Life

to the delight of other children in the home, foods they especially enjoyed. This information was shared with other class members later when meals were prepared and delivered to the home immediately before and after the delivery. Other Stork Team members helped with housecleaning and care for the mom-to-be's small children during her doctor visits or just to allow her time to rest. Ministry to the family continued for several weeks after the birth. This ad-hoc team was the catalyst for involving many class members in ministry.

Sunday School and Worship

Participation in classes and departments or other Bible study groups provides opportunities for people to worship through prayer and praise; express stewardship of time, abilities, and resources; and otherwise express devotion to God. Sunday School can emphasize the need to seek God's power and presence by seeking Him.

Leaders must set aside time daily in their lives to remember who God is and to seek Him through personal prayer and Bible study. Teachers and leaders also encourage participants in their groups to do the same.

Establish an environment in Bible study groups that lead people to encounter and respond to the life-changing God through the study of His Word in the fellowship of His people. Such an environment will help your people open their lives to God. When they do, amazing things will happen! Evangelism becomes a priority, fellowship grows, discipleship deepens, and ministry multiplies!

Communicating a Vision of Sunday School as a Major Method of Your Church's Open Groups Strategy

A church that intends to carry out the Great Commission mandate to "make disciples" must have a way to encounter the spiritually lost to lead them to an encounter with God in Christ. As noted, a key church practice strategy in the Kingdom-Focused Church Model and Process for doing that is the open group strategy. Most churches already have in place the best organizational framework for this strategy: Sunday School, or whatever you call your church's ongoing Bible study ministry. Six descriptors characterize the strategy message of open groups. Note how each is evident in Sunday School ministry.

Foundational

The open group serves as a basic entry point into the church for unbelievers. Yes, unbelievers can and do enter the life of a church in other ways, but the open group is intentionally designed to target the unbeliever. Sunday School as an open-group methodology is a foundational ministry for helping a church do the work of the Great Commission.

45

ESSENTIALS FOR EXCELLENCE

Perhaps the most common illustration is the foundation of a building. A solid foundation is critical to the stability of any structure. It comes first because the rest of the structure is built on it and supported by it. The framework for the rest of the building is attached to it. No wise builder begins with walls. Obviously the roof is not constructed first. Similarly, Sunday School is a starting place for a church that wants to develop a comprehensive approach for reaching the spiritually lost and moving them toward mature discipleship.

On the other hand, a foundation without walls or a roof is incomplete. So it is with Sunday School ministry. A Sunday School, especially one with an open-group mind-set, that is not attached to a strategy for discipling new believers and equipping leaders will eventually become dysfunctional.

Sunday School is foundational evangelism, in that it has the objective of leading people to faith in the Lord Jesus Christ. Leaders are enlisted, organization is developed, leader training is provided, and teaching is focused to achieve this evangelistic objective. Sunday School is foundational discipleship because it builds on-mission Christians. The emphasis on ongoing, systematic Bible study is a first step in the maturation process of the believer.

Ongoing

Living for Jesus is a daily commitment. Included in that commitment is obedience to His commands. At least one of His commands is to "make disciples." To be a faithful follower, then, calls for a strategy that leads us into an ongoing effort to lead people to faith in Christ.

Sunday School meets the criteria. As a meeting time, Sunday School in most church settings meets weekly. Sunday School takes no vacations; it is solid, stable, dependable, and reliable. It has a proven track record over time.

Sunday School ministry is ongoing in the scope of the work. Sunday School is at work in the lives of members and leaders 24-7.

Evangelistic

The open-group strategy exists to lead people to faith in the Lord Jesus Christ. It serves as a primary entry point into the church for unbelievers. "An open group is an eternal touch point where the lost of the world come together with the saved of the world so that the Savior of the world can advance His kingdom by bringing people to salvation."[3]

Sunday School leaders and members must be dedicated to seeking, discovering, and inviting spiritually lost people to participate in the Bible study groups. In addition, leaders and members work one-on-one to interact with the spiritually lost in settings away from the church and to present the good news of Jesus to them. An evangelistic Sunday School takes seriously the responsibility of witnessing to others through evangelistic teaching and evangelistic visitation, both as a group and as an individual response to the Great Commission.

Connecting Sunday School to Life

Bible Study

The vehicle for carrying out the open group strategy is a Bible study group, which by definition is intentionally *evangelistic* Bible study. These individual units are where the personal touch takes place.

The primary question in these groups is, What is God saying to us through the Bible text? The Bible is the focus of the study, in comparison to groups that gather primarily for support, fellowship, or leadership development.

The Bible is the written record of God's revelation of Himself. The Bible alone shows the way of salvation. It provides the answer to the deepest need of all humanity: atonement for sin. Salvation and atonement are made possible through God's redemptive work of mercy and grace, which reached its fulfillment in the sending of His Son, Jesus, to die for our sin. From Sunday School's beginnings on the streets of Gloucester, England, 220 years ago, the Bible has been the centerpiece for teaching in Sunday School.

Bible study groups that are designed primarily for reaching lost people are open groups. Bible study groups that are designed primarily for moving saved people toward spiritual maturity and transformation are closed groups.

Intentional Mix of Believers and Unbelievers

An open group strategy is built around intentional evangelistic Bible study designed to help the unbeliever come to know Christ. Of course, that assumes the presence of unbelievers, but not just because they happened to come; someone invited them to come. The believer's role is to invite the unbeliever, to model what it means to live as a follower of Christ, and, through the Bible study, to be equipped to witness for Christ in all of life's settings. An all-age Sunday School ministry provides a place for everyone: all are invited, all may come, all are wanted.

Sunday School is a powerful force for evangelistic witness, nurture, and ministry. Here are some reasons this is true:

- The organizational structure of small groups encourages and supports personal interaction with unbelievers.
- Witnessing is identified as a clear responsibility of Sunday School leaders and members.[4]
- Sunday School ministry is always on call. (See "Ongoing.")
- Sunday School ministry teaches evangelistically as appropriate for the age group.
- Sunday School ministry generally has the largest leader and member base, giving it unparalleled potential impact.

Who else can reach the spiritually lost with the good news of Christ except those individuals who know Him personally and have experienced personally the efficacy of the message? The role of the disciple is clear and the work

inescapable. We are to make disciples. How can that be done effectively and intentionally if we do not interact with the lost? Therefore, "Go!"

Multiplication

The potential of the strategy increases with every new evangelistic Bible study group. Therefore, the strategy depends on an intentional plan to increase units and leaders for those units.

These groups, commonly referred to as *classes and departments*, are the individual units where the personal touch takes place. In these groups people are mobilized to work. The number of groups in the complete organization or any age-group portion thereof is based on the sound principles that characterize an age-graded organization.

Of course, if the number of organizational units increases, then the leadership base also needs to increase. But we are not just talking about filling positions. The leaders of Sunday School open Bible study groups must understand why those groups exist, how they function, and what is expected of them as leaders. Therefore, discovering, enlisting, and training Sunday School leaders as kingdom leaders are important tasks in a church that is relying on Sunday School as its open group methodology.

Here are reasons to make multiplication of leaders and units a priority:

- Birthing new Sunday School units creates excitement.
- As the organization is enlarged, new growth takes place naturally.
- New units tend to grow more quickly than existing units.
- New units are easier for newcomers to penetrate.
- New leaders and members of new units tend to be more aggressive in evangelism and ministry.
- New units provide more opportunities for people to serve.

Communicating the Vision in Personal Terms

My neighbor, Bill Swanson, is lost. How do I know? He told me. Bill is lost and bound for hell, and he really doesn't care. Let me also tell you that Bill is a great guy. You'd like him! He and his wife, Karen, are a great couple and good neighbors. As I have built a relationship with Bill and shared with him how he can have eternal life through Christ, his response was, "That's well and good for you and your family. That's just not for me."

There likely are many "Bills" in your circle of influence: work associates, neighbors, a close relative, parents of children on your kid's soccer team. These people know nothing of God's love, grace, forgiveness, or eternal life. Take a few minutes to put a name to those "Bills" you know:

Connecting Sunday School to Life

Oh, how we need to remind one another that people all around us are lost. All that we do in church, all that is at the heart of Sunday School ministry, all that we call our vision, all the plans we make—everything is to be directed toward fulfilling the kingdom mandate to make disciples of lost people like Bill Swanson.

People like Bill help to give our vision a name and a face. We are about more than "church work"; we are about kingdom work. It is the work Jesus was about when He said, "The time is fulfilled, and the kingdom of God has come near: Repent and believe in the good news" (Mark 1:15). He had a kingdom vision; He lived a kingdom vision. So must we.

---

[1]Norman Shawchuck and Roger Heuser, *Leading the Congregation: Caring for Yourself While Serving the People* (Nashville: Abingdon Press, 1993), 142-43.

[2]Sunday School ministry is a strategy for doing the work of the church, not an organization to be treated as a separate entity. Therefore, in many ways references to Sunday School are to be understood as references to the church.

[3]Gene Mims, *Kingdom Principles for Church Growth, Revised and Expanded* (Nashville: LifeWay Press, 2001), 102.

[4]For information about the FAITH Sunday School Evangelism Strategy®, call toll free 1-877-324-8498, refer to the e-book on this book's CD-ROM or visit LifeWay.com.

Historical purpose of ss. evangelism
success   "   "
Mechanism
Focused Bible study
Intentional mix of believers & unsaved.
"   plan to increase class units & leaders
Leadership Understanding @ 48
Reasons for Multiplication @ 48

SECTION 2

Developing a Kingdom Vision for Sunday School Ministry

Why does your church have Sunday School? The responses I hear when I ask this question in conferences include *Bible study, fellowship, to meet the needs of the members,* and *to reach people.* Someone always gives this answer, too: *"We have Sunday School at our church because we have always had it."*

Many things happen in churches today under the guise of "Sunday School." For what purposes does your church have Sunday School? So members can go deeper in their study of the Scriptures? To strengthen the fellowship of the congregation? To meet physical, emotional, and social needs?

Does your Sunday School exist as a place where unchurched and unsaved people can learn about the kingdom of God? If Sunday School is to help the church accomplish kingdom work, then members of Bible study groups must be challenged to serve Christ and follow His example. They must be organized for service, equipped for every good work, and mobilized for ministry. Sunday School must be seen not as a program or an organization but as a strategy your church can use to achieve its vision.

Sunday School is the foundational strategy in a local church for leading people to faith in the Lord Jesus Christ and for building on-mission Christians through open Bible study groups that engage people in evangelism, discipleship, fellowship, ministry, and worship. When seen as part of the church's open group strategy, Sunday School becomes a means of guiding people to come to know Jesus and deepen their lives in evangelism, discipleship, fellowship, ministry, and worship. Knowing Jesus and learning what it means to follow Him are life-changing experiences! These outcomes also are goals of the teaching in Sunday Schools that are vehicles for an open group strategy.

If your Sunday School is to fulfill its objective as your church's main open group strategy, then as a leader you must champion and communicate the objective in a clear, compelling way. These strategic principles, foundational to Sunday School ministry, provide a good way to do so. (For details, see *Ten Best Practices to Make Your Sunday School Work.*)

The Principle of Foundational Evangelism
The Principle of Foundational Discipleship
The Principle of Family Responsibility
The Principle of Spiritual Transformation
The Principle of Biblical Leadership

Ten Best Practices of Sunday School (CD-ROM)

The ten best practices are based on observing churches that have effectively used Sunday School in a strategic way. Their effectiveness is realized in the commitment of the people to the mission of Christ, the willingness of people to work, and of course, the quickening power of the Holy Spirit. Apart from the Spirit, no lasting kingdom work takes place.

Because the primary focus of this book is on vision, greater attention is given in the following section to those practices that can help you plan or organize accordingly. All ten best practices deserve your balanced attention, so use this resource alongside *Ten Best Practices*.

1. COMMIT TO THE STRATEGY.

We commit to Sunday School as the foundational strategy in our church for doing the work of the Great Commission.

Commitment Through an Annual Plan

One way to express this commitment is to develop an annual plan. Clear vision and a great strategy will get you nowhere unless you properly execute a well-developed plan. Planning is probably the hardest part of the work. As a leader you may have a good idea of where your church needs to go and what it needs to do to get there. You can even envision the results. But developing the step-by-step process of getting from point A to point B is what is needed.

Annual planning takes time and energy, but saves time later and brings long-term positive results. The annual planning process is the first step toward closing the gap between where your church is now and where you want to be. (For other benefits of annual planning, see the **CD-ROM**.)

Where is our church now? _____

Where do we want to be by the end of the year? _____

_____

Measure your planning by what you want to accomplish. Your church might do many good things that do not contribute to your vision. Focus *all* your attention on what you want your church to do through Sunday School.

Conduct an annual planning event. Annual planning is best done by a team. In many churches the team that develops the annual detail of the strategy—the strategic plan—is called the *Sunday School planning team.* The composition of that team may vary depending on the size of your church and the organizational structure used to group people for Bible study.

For example, your team may consist of the pastor, education staff, general leaders, and division directors. If the church only has age-group departments, the planning team may consist of the pastor, education staff, general leaders, and department directors. In smaller churches or churches with a class structure, the team may include the pastor, Sunday School director, and a leader from each class.

Whatever the composition, this team is responsible for leading the planning process and formulates details of the strategy. This work can be done during an annual planning event. Here are some steps to prepare for that event.

Set the date. Many churches do their annual planning in the spring for the church year that begins in the fall. Consider doing your annual planning far enough in advance to affect organizational, space, and leadership needs. It is helpful to complete enlistment so that new Sunday School leaders can be involved in developing the plans they will help implement.

Determine the schedule. Several schedules are possible for your annual planning event. Choose one of the following or, better yet, create your own. Another option is to spread agenda items over several weeknight sessions.

Friday-Saturday Retreat

Friday

6:00 p.m.	Supper
7:00	Welcome
	• What We Hope to Accomplish
	• Agenda Review
7:15	Devotional on the Great Commission
	• Prayer for God's Leadership
	• Sunday School: Our Church's Great Commission Strategy
8:00	A Look at Where We Are—Evaluation
9:30	Dismiss

(handwritten notes): —No. new classes started   1 per 12 mo.-baptisms -Children -Youth -Adult   Avg Attendance by Month -Preschool -Children -Youth -Adult

Saturday

8:00 a.m.	Breakfast
8:45	Devotional
9:00	A Look at What Our Evaluation Shows Us—Our Needs
10:30	Break
10:45	Setting Priorities and Determining Goals
Noon	Lunch
12:45 p.m.	Building Action Plans
3:00	Committing Our Plans to God
3:30	Dismiss and Head Home

All-Day Saturday Retreat

8:30 a.m.	Continental Breakfast
9:00	Welcome
	• What We Hope to Accomplish
	• Agenda Review
9:15	Devotional on the Great Commission
	• Prayer for God's Leadership
	• Sunday School: Our Church's Great Commission Strategy
10:00	A Look at Where We Are—Evaluation
11:00	A Look at What Our Evaluation Shows Us—Our Needs
Noon	Lunch
12:45 p.m.	Setting Priorities and Determining Goals
1:30	Building Action Plans
3:30	Committing Our Plans to God
3:45	Dismiss and Head Home

Connecting Sunday School to Life

Secure a location. Select a location that allows everyone to avoid distractions, helps them to focus their thinking, and stimulates creativity. Options include an associational or state convention assembly or encampment, a local hotel/motel conference room, a state park, a member's vacation cabin, a neighboring church facility, or the home of a planning team member.

If none of these options is possible, your church building can be a good location. You have easy access to records and can view space and equipment. If you meet at the church, find ways to make the meeting extraordinary.

Wherever you meet, provide an atmosphere that is conducive to good planning. Tables facilitate looking at materials and taking notes. Provide comfortable chairs. A white board or overhead projector to record comments and brainstorm ideas is a good addition to the room. As the event leader, arrive early to finalize room arrangements and make sure everything is in order.

Make resources available. Your annual planning event can be enhanced by having these resources on hand:

Planning Guide—One purpose of this resource is to help you plan. Do not overlook the vast amount of information on this **CD-ROM.** Other resources include your Bible, *Ten Best Practices,* and resources that treat Sunday School as strategy.

Records—Provide a summary of enrollment and attendance records for each class and department. Gather other information that helps leaders answer these questions:

- What was the total Bible study enrollment at the beginning of the year? the end of the year? How many people were enrolled during the year? How many were dropped?
- What was the annual net gain or loss?
- What was the total average attendance this year? The previous year?
- For the year, how many contacts for each class and department were reported? How many visitors?
- Are there any known deficiencies in record-keeping that may affect the accuracy of these statistics?

Provide 5- and 10-year summaries—perhaps in a graph or chart—that show total enrollment, new people enrolled, names dropped, and average attendance. Training records, such as your church's Christian Growth Study Plan summary, will also prove helpful information for planning.

Calendars—Obtain copies of the church, associational, state convention, and SBC calendars. Identify possible leadership development events at LifeWay Glorieta and LifeWay Ridgecrest Conference Centers. Pull dates that relate to your plans and compile them for use during planning sessions.

Budget—During annual planning you will begin to formulate a budget to carry out your Sunday School strategy. Budget and expenditure information for the current and previous years will be helpful. Of course, a new budget

needs to reflect the plans being made for the year ahead, not simply be adjusted from last year. The Budget Planning Worksheet on the **CD-ROM** may be used.

Goals—Review goals that were set for the current year. This evaluation can be helpful as you anticipate setting goals for the new church year.

Organizational Information—A major subject of discussion during annual planning will be the structure of the Bible teaching organization for the coming year. Use the current list of classes and departments, enrollment and average attendance totals, and prospect information to help leaders determine where new departments or classes might be needed.

Prospect/Potential Member Information—To know the number of prospects (and their status) is helpful in projecting goals, as well as for making plans for evangelism, enrollment, leader enlistment, new units, budget, and so forth.

Plan actions to achieve goals. The planning process is incomplete unless it results in determining specific actions to achieve goals. An action plan, to be built for each goal, should identify the actions to be taken, the persons responsible, and the dates by which actions are to be completed. Action plans can be very specific; for example, "Order appropriate-size chairs for the Twos-Threes department" (see the **CD-ROM** for a sample Strategic Plan Sheet). Here are some terms to remember as you develop your strategic plans.

- *Objectives* are broad statements that declare the long-term intent of your Sunday School ministry.
- *Goals* are focused, short-term statements that can be used to track progress toward an objective.
- *Actions* are specific, intentional steps toward accomplishing a goal.

Give annual planning your best effort, as it will help accomplish your vision for what God wants you to do. Pray for His guidance at each step of the way.

Ongoing Sunday School Planning Team Meetings

All of the planning required to accomplish your vision cannot take place in a single annual planning event. Plans need to be reviewed and new situations addressed. Your Sunday School planning team (the same people who are on the annual planning team) should determine a time to meet monthly. By meeting regularly, the Sunday School planning team positions itself to be proactive. The team can purposefully look for ways to move the plan ahead. Crisis responses become less the norm.

Select an appropriate meeting time. A Sunday School planning team meeting following the last Sunday of the month is ideal because statistical data for the month usually is available. The members of the team need to select the time most convenient for them. Usually one hour is sufficient.

Use an agenda. Preparing and distributing an agenda before the meeting reminds participants of the time and place, identifies the focus of the meeting, provides a summary of the work to be completed, and clarifies responsibilities.

[handwritten note in left margin: who should be on the SS planning team / which mtgs monthly]

Connecting Sunday School to Life

Follow up after the meeting. Send a summary so absentees will know what occurred during the meeting and those who attended will recall assignments.

Just as it is important for the planning team to meet often, it is even more critical for all Sunday School leaders to meet. The benefits of weekly or monthly meetings for all leaders is addressed in Build Kingdom Leaders.

2. ORGANIZE WITH PURPOSE.

We organize our Sunday School ministry to accomplish the objectives of leading people to faith in the Lord Jesus Christ and building on-mission Christians.

Simply stated, *organization* is placing ourselves in the best possible position to be used by the Holy Spirit. Each piece of the organization is to fit together in such a way that the whole can operate smoothly and effectively to accomplish its intended purpose.

Purpose and *vision* are key words. You do not fit your vision to the organization; rather, you structure your organization to allow the vision to be achieved. Your Sunday School vision needs to influence why and how you develop your Sunday School organization. When the structure ceases to support the strategy, then the structure should be changed.

Sunday School as strategy is implemented by clustering people into groups primarily based on age. The importance of the organizational unit cannot be overemphasized. These individual units are where the personal touch takes place—where needs are met, relationships are built, and individuals can mature in their relationship to Christ through ongoing study of God's Word. See Sunday School Strategy Growth Worksheet (pp. 32-33 and **CD-ROM**).

Age Grading

Few things in Baptist life in general and Sunday School in particular create as much anxiety as organizing by age. I once heard a story of a Sunday School director who worked as sports editor for the local paper. One night he dreamed he was walking through a cemetery and came across a headstone with his name on it. The inscription read:

> *Here lie the bones of Jimmy Lee. For him life held no terror.*
> *His death the result of age grading adults—no hits, no runs, no errors!*

Grading the Preschool through Student Divisions has become fairly standardized using the public educational system as a model and making adaptations for church size. But what about adults? Adults are independent, married, single, raising families, working, retired, and so forth. Do they need someone to tell them which class to attend?

How shall we teach adults as we grow?

Some system must be in place for organizing adults or the Bible study ministry will stagnate. Using age as the organizing principle has proven to be the best—even for adults!

Perhaps the label has become the handicap. *Targeting adult groups* is better than *age grading* and accomplishes the same purpose. A church can "target" single adults who are in a specific age range or "target" all adults—single or married—within a specific age range. Many churches have successfully overcome the age-grading barrier by using this concept. Here's an example.

Target Age Group: Adults 25-35 Years of Age

Within this age range are many options for affinity groups. Classes can be structured based on the life station of group members. Consider the possibilities:

- Single Adults
- Married Adults
- Formerly Married Adults
- Married, No Children
- Single, No Children
- Adults (Married and Single), with Preschoolers
- Married, with Preschoolers
- Singles, with Preschoolers
- Adults (Married and Single), with Children
- Married, with Children
- Singles, with Children
- Adults (Married and Single), with Teenagers
- Married, with Teenagers
- Singles, with Teenagers
- Women's Class
- Men's Class

While not exhaustive, this list gives you an idea of possible groupings. Choose any combination to form a class or department. An example of a department based on targeting adults in this age group could include these organizations:

- Married Adults, Ages 25-35
- Women, Ages 25-35
- Men, Ages 25-35
- Singles, Ages 25-35

An even simpler version would be:

- Coed Adults, Ages 25-35
- Women, Ages 25-35
- Men, Ages 25-35

Dwayne McCrary, minister to young adults and discipleship at First Baptist Church, Lubbock, Texas, is committed to starting new adult Bible study units this way. He has classes for young adults with preschoolers, young adults with children, young adults with teens, and so forth. Dwayne emails:

We have already added three new classes in the Young Married Adult Division and are about to add a fourth. Our numbers have increased by about 40 on average; the numbers coincide with the number of classes we added. We have increased by 10 people for every class we have started, just like the rule says!

The interesting thing is that teachers have taken the initiative. In every case the teacher approached the director and then me to say a class had gotten so large that we needed to start a new one to continue to grow! New teachers are recruited by current teachers, who leave to start the new classes. Talk about fun! Organizing this way has made a significant difference and has given us some flexibility within general guidelines.

Grade your Sunday School in the way that best enables you to fulfill your vision. Remember these organizing principles:

• Keep the structure simple enough for everyone to understand. Instead of using names for classes, use age or target groups instead. When a first-timer age 34 visits, it is easier for him to find and identify with a Coed Class for Ages 25-35 than the Faithful Friends class.
• Make the organization comprehensive enough to include everyone who presently attends or should be reached by your church.
• Be flexible enough to grow with your church.
• Make the reason for creating new units obvious.
• Allow for natural movement from one class or age group to another.
• Maximize growth principles by making the organization practical.

Grouping by Study Topic

A popular option is grouping adults by topical interests or needs. While appropriate for short-term studies, this approach has weaknesses:

• Interest-based groups tend to focus on the personality of the teacher.
• These groups quickly become "unopen" groups. Once a study is under way it is difficult for newcomers to penetrate the groups.
• The need to change topics regularly requires constant reorganization, and finding new and interesting topics becomes more difficult as time passes.
• Constant change makes it difficult to build relationships.
• The organization can become difficult to explain to first-time attenders.

Some churches use interest-based groups as entry points into the church's Bible study ministry. For example, a single parent attends a short-term topical group on parenting. Through that encounter she is enrolled in Bible study, where she accepts Christ as Savior and begins her journey of discipleship.

To use interest-based groups effectively as entry points, there should be a stated end point. Leaders should be committed to transitioning participants to ongoing Bible study groups at the end of the study.

3. BUILD KINGDOM LEADERS.

We build leaders who demonstrate a commitment to the kingdom, Christ as Lord, the ministry to which they have been called, the church, and the mission mandate Christ has given.

The Holy Spirit has given every Christian at least one spiritual gift to be used for the common good (1 Cor. 12:7). At least one objective of the Sunday School enlistment process is to help individuals find ways to use that gift in service to Christ, His church, and others.

Ultimately, the goal is to identify, enlist, and build people into kingdom leaders. "A kingdom leader can be defined as a person called by God to follow Christ in a life of discipleship, utilizing the leadership gifts given by the Holy Spirit to lead the church in carrying out the Great Commission for the purpose of expanding the kingdom of God."[1] This type of leader becomes the lesson lived out in the crucibles of life.

The importance of a church's closed-group strategy cannot be overemphasized. An effective closed-group strategy provides a base of leaders from which to identify and enlist people to serve in Sunday School.

Discovery and Enlistment

Begin with prayer. The harvest and the workers are His, and God is the One who sends them out (Matt. 9:37-38). We need to depend on Him when we enlist leaders. The first step, then, is sincere, fervent, and seeking prayer.

Search the church membership rolls. Sunday School leaders need to be church members. Potential leaders often identified from the church roll include VBS workers, college graduates returning home, leader development course participants, referrals from adult teachers, current Sunday School associates or apprentices, retirees, public- and private-sector schoolteachers, former Sunday School leaders not currently working, and respondents to interest surveys.

Identify positions to be filled. Start with the most critical positions. Be careful not to fill a position just because it is important and vacant. Filling a position does not guarantee that the work will be done.

Identify spiritual gifts. Several resources can help leaders discover and analyze spiritual giftedness, including the S.E.RV.E. inventory (**CD-ROM**).

Identify leader relationships. Leaders should be interviewed and enlisted by the person to whom they will be responsible. In other words, whomever the new leader would call if he or she were unable to be present on Sunday is the individual who should make the enlistment visit.

Decide on one person. Contact the one person God is leading you to enlist. Avoid developing a backup list in case someone turns you down. If you have sought the God's will and believe that God wants you to ask a certain person to serve in a certain position, a backup list is probably not needed!

Connecting Sunday School to Life

Make an enlistment visit (**CD-ROM**). Communicate the importance of the work by enlisting Sunday School teachers privately. If a home visit is not appropriate, make an appointment to talk privately at church. Address any safety and security issues at enlistment. For a Volunteer Leader Screening Form, see the **CD-ROM**.

Identifying the Sunday School Leadership Team

The Sunday School leadership team consists of everyone who has been enlisted as a Sunday School leader in any age group. Everyone is on the same team, working to implement the Sunday School vision. All leaders deserve to know the expectations and responsibilities of their roles. When leaders understand what they are supposed to do and see they are part of a team, they are more likely to respond positively to the call to serve. Leadership Team job descriptions (**CD-ROM**) suggest major responsibilities for each position.

Building Leaders Through Weekly Leadership Meetings

The weekly leadership meeting can help all Sunday School leaders be more effective in all aspects of Sunday School ministry. The meeting provides a regular time for leaders to focus on the vision, on relationships, and on life-changing Bible study. For extensive help on leadership meetings and a training needs survey, see the **CD-ROM**.

4. DEVELOP SOUL-WINNERS.

We lead all leaders and members to become soul-winners and witnesses for Christ in all life settings, including the home.

One unifying theme throughout Scripture is God's initiative to redeem sinful humanity. His unchanging desire is that everyone be saved. His loving purpose reached its zenith in sending Jesus Christ, His Son, as the sacrifice for the sin of the world. Following His resurrection, the Lord commissioned His followers to bear witness to what God had made possible in Christ.

Here are some reasons Sunday School is the best vehicle for driving a church to achieve its evangelistic vision.

- Sunday School open Bible study groups are prepared to reach, teach, witness, and disciple through teachers and ministry coordinators, as well as visitation-evangelism coordinators and care group leaders, depending on class size. Another evangelism or outreach ministry is not needed.
- Sunday School is structured into small groups where individual caring and reaching can take place.
- Witnessing is a clear responsibility of leaders and members.
- By functioning every week, Sunday School is a stable and reliable ministry designed to witness about Jesus and to teach God's Word.

- Sunday School has the largest number of leaders (approximately one million) and participants of any church ministry. The potential impact on a lost world is staggering!

Many Sunday School leaders and members will never effectively share the gospel because they are not trained to do so. Thousands of churches can testify to the effectiveness of the FAITH Sunday School Evangelism Strategy® in changing lives—those touched by the powerful gospel message and those who stepped out to share it. FAITH is supported in LifeWay Sunday School resources. (See the FAITH e-book on the **CD-ROM.**)

5. WIN THE LOST.

We engage in evangelistic actions that result in winning the lost to Christ as well as in other actions that focus on the unchurched and reclaim the spiritually indifferent.

An age-graded Sunday School provides the best structure for organizing a church's evangelistic, outreach, and ministry visitation effort.

Preschool Sunday School leaders visit preschool-age children to help cultivate relationships with the child and maximize teaching opportunities. In visiting the child, the preschool teacher may have opportunities to witness and minister to unsaved parents and other family members. The same is true of visits made to younger children. (See preschool and children's e-books on the **CD-ROM.**)

Older children should be visited by Children's Sunday School leaders even if the family receives a visit from adult class representatives. If the child attended Sunday School alone, obtain permission from the parent or guardian before making a visit. Children's leaders need to be trained to share the gospel with older children and prepared to talk to adults in the home.

Students in grades 7-12 may have a specific time for participating in evangelistic and ministry visitation to other teenagers. In most cases students need to be trained to give an evangelistic witness and be accompanied by adult leaders trained to share the gospel. (Student FAITH may be an option.)

Adult evangelistic and ministry visits should be made by teams from the Bible study group or class to which the unbeliever or member is assigned. Consider having a team from every group participate in visitation. A ministry coordinator/visitation-evangelism coordinator leads the class's visitation efforts.

Develop and maintain a prospect file and a membership file as part of recording, distributing, and receiving information about people. The prospect file will help you determine the growth potential of your church; the number of prospects on file should equal your Sunday School enrollment. Several options are available—card files and preprinted assignment forms, a pocket-and-card system, or electronic files and computer-generated assignment forms.

These elements should be part of any prospect file system.

A master file—This permanent file is where all information about each prospect or member is logged and tracked. For every person it is helpful to have name, address, phone number, email address, class/department, spiritual condition (believer or unbeliever), and other desired information.

This file may be arranged alphabetically by family units or by individuals. Other options include geographical areas and age groups. You may choose more than one approach—a family master file and an age-group master file. Remember that these are master files, not working files for assignments!

Keep a separate file for prospects and for members. Make sure the member file can be accessed by Sunday School division, department, and class leaders.

Working files for assignments. These are the files from which assignments are made and on which members make notes about visits. New or corrected information needs to be recorded so both the working file and the master file can be updated each week. Each Sunday School class and department must have access to information regarding people who would relate to this file.

Someone from the church office should maintain master and working files. This person should receive and update information each week, distribute updated information in time for weekly leadership meetings, prepare visitation assignment cards based on updated information, and assign prospects to the appropriate class or department.

Follow a standard assignment process. Every first-time attender and prospect should be assigned to a Sunday School class or department. In case of family prospects, assignments can be made to adult classes and classes of preschoolers, children, or students. Leaders coordinate visits and contacts.

6. ASSIMILATE PEOPLE

We assimilate individuals and families into the life of the church and facilitate their growth as disciples of Christ.

Assimilation is the process of moving a new member to a heart-deep level of commitment to and involvement in the church. Every church with a heart for evangelism and church health must be concerned about assimilation.

Evangelistic results do not automatically translate into church growth. Some churches report a large number of conversions but show little increase in Bible study attendance, giving, or other measures of a healthy church. This pattern suggests that those being won to Christ are not being assimilated into the body.

Assimilation is more than becoming a member. Someone can be a church member but never feel assimilated into the body. The goal is to help people feel that they are wanted, that they belong, and that they are needed.

ESSENTIALS FOR EXCELLENCE

Assimilation helps members know where they can serve the body of Christ (see 1 Cor. 12). Spiritual assessment instruments like S.E.R.V.E. (**CD-ROM**) can help new members understand and use their spiritual gifts.

Assimilation cannot be accomplished without some small-group process. A church may do well at attracting people through dynamic worship or other avenues; but if people are to feel wanted and needed, they need the relationships that are developed in small groups. Your Sunday School ministry with its small, open Bible study groups provides the most comprehensive system for ensuring that everyone has that type of experience.

Assimilation is a process that enables members to express interest in a new member and new members to experience that interest from others. A goal is to lead new members to the point that they begin assimilating new members. Here are suggestions to move new members toward such a heart-deep commitment.

Enlist class greeters. Every class or group should have someone at the door to greet guests. This is one of the most important leadership roles in a class. Some guests will find their way to a classroom; others may be brought by someone from the church's welcome center. No matter how they get there, walking into a roomful of strangers is intimidating. A greeter can help guests feel welcome and, by introducing them to others, ease them into the group.

Use name tags for everyone. Knowing people's names indicates that you have enough interest to remember who they are. Being addressed personally says that someone considers you to be significant. Name tags help people get to know one another and enable leaders to call everyone by name. And yes, everyone, even members, should wear name tags (and yes, every week!).

When my family moved to Nashville, we immediately began looking for a church home. In several churches, the welcome center provided name tags for us to wear. When we arrived at the adult class, however, we were the only ones wearing a name tag. Picture the scenario: We are in a class for the first time, attempting to remember the names of 15-20 people. The class members have only two names to remember; yet, we were the only ones with name tags!

Use get-acquainted activities. Newcomers can complete open-ended comments as, "I came to Sunday School the first time because . . .", sharing what they like about the church. In the case of adults and students, groups of three or four members (or couples) can facilitate informal get-togethers once a month or quarter outside of Sunday morning Bible study.

Maximize Sunday morning Bible study for assimilation. Sunday mornings provide an opportunity for members and guests to enjoy Christian fellowship. People visit informally before and after the session.

Participation in Bible study becomes a bond. Teachers should look for opportunities to have the class form smaller groups to respond to questions or complete a leader guide activity. When small groups of two or three discuss a question, they not only discover biblical truth they also get to know one another better.

Celebrate special occasions. By celebrating birthdays in a simple way, you affirm everyone (don't omit anyone). Consider monthly birthday fellowships.

Plan social events. Don't overlook the obvious. Every newcomer, new member, and guest should be invited to every social event or fellowship. Enlist someone to "adopt" newcomers in order to introduce them to class members and to involve them in different aspects of the event.

Develop and use mentors. In adult and student classes, a spiritually mature class member may be assigned to encourage a new member in his or her spiritual growth and development.

7. PARTNER WITH FAMILIES.

We partner with parents and families to build the home as the center of biblical guidance.

Whose responsibility is it to teach family members the Bible? According to Deuteronomy 6:6-9, parents are charged by God to quote His Word, read it aloud, explain it, discuss it, symbolize it, write it down, and so incorporate it into the fiber of their lives that their children will see the value of godly living. In short, parents are to assume the responsibility of being the primary Bible teachers and disciplers of the children.

You can encourage families to read and study the Bible together. Family Bible Time EXTRA! at LifeWay.com, is a great tool for a family Bible study.

For most people, their closest relationship, either in physical proximity or emotional quality, are family members. A family can be strengthened by a family member who consistently engages in individual Bible study. Families sometimes come under the influence of a church's ministry and into right relationship with the Lord because a family member is reached:

• When a child is the first to attend church, 3.5 percent of families follow.
• When a wife or mother is the first to attend church, 17 percent of families follow.
• When a dad or husband is the first to attend church, 93 percent of families follow.[2]

8. TEACH TO TRANSFORM.

We engage individuals and families in the biblical model of instruction that leads to spiritual transformation.

Exposing people, both lost and saved, to God's Word so their hearts and minds might be transformed in Christ is what Sunday School is all about! The ultimate goal is that all leaders and learners integrate in their hearts and minds the biblical truth that sets the course for living. Spiritual transformation begins when a spiritually lost person repents and places personal faith in

Christ. It continues as the believer lives out his new identity in Christ in obedience to God's Word.

Teaching to transform lives can move your Sunday School to become all that God intends it to be. Open Bible study groups can become the vehicle for engaging people in the work of the church—evangelism, discipleship, fellowship, ministry, and worship. Consequently, the Bible study class should not exist solely as a teaching group but should also focus on discipling, caring, and so forth. All of the work should be kept in balance, and the teacher is the leader who ensures that this balance is maintained.

Do not enlist teachers solely on the basis of their Bible knowledge and ability to communicate. While these elements are important, the teacher needs to see himself as the catalyst for leading the class to fulfill its purpose.

A Sunday School teacher should be characterized by some nonnegotiable traits: (1) articulates clear testimony of a personal relationship with Jesus Christ; (2) actively shares his faith with others; (3) models a Christian home; (4) gives evidence of spending time alone with God; and (5) shows commitment to the church through worship, stewardship, and other support. (See Section 3 and the **CD-ROM** e-books.)

9. MOBILIZE FOR MINISTRY.

We take deliberate actions to mobilize people to meet with compassion the needs of individuals and families.

I hope this book has challenged the thinking that Sunday School only happens on Sunday! No strategy built on the Great Commission can be accomplished in only one hour a week. Throughout the New Testament we see Jesus calling for a lifetime commitment. He also modeled ministry and humble service (Mark 10:45; John 13:12-15).

The 24-7 aspect of Sunday School is especially true with ministry. In this context, ministry is people helping other people in Jesus' name to meet the needs of life that they often cannot meet themselves. Every class, no matter the age group, should be organized for the personal care of all members.

"Organize with Purpose" (pp. 57-59) offers help in developing an adult class structure. The various roles of the organization are designed to facilitate ministry as well as outreach and teaching. If you have large classes, you may need to take additional steps to ensure that ministry takes place consistently. Remember that the ability to assemble a large group for Bible study is not the final objective. An open Bible study group is a vehicle for leading people to do what the church does. One principle function of the church is ministry.

The development of ministry subgroups or teams becomes more critical the larger the class grows. Leaders of large classes need to be team players who understand the Sunday School vision and are committed to carrying it out.

The most successful approach involves class ministry coordinators and care group leaders who are enlisted to care for a specific number of prospects and members. The primary responsibility is to care for the needs of those assigned—not only absentees but also those who attend every week. Here are some actions these leaders may take with their ministry groups:

Maintain contact with group members through telephone calls, emails, and personal notes.

Make a personal visit to every new member assigned. The initial visit may be to get to know the person and provide encouragement to be a vital participant in the ministry group and the Sunday School class.

Make personal visits as ministry needs and special occasions occur.

Send personal notes or cards to acknowledge special occasions.

Keep records of visits, calls, and other contacts. Include information about ministry needs, prayer concerns, and ministry actions.

As appropriate, share prayer and ministry needs with the class. In most cases, the class needs to be involved in prayer and response to needs. In some situations, however, a ministry leader may learn things that are not to be shared and should be treated with confidentiality. Breaking confidences will hinder future ministry opportunities.

Pass on ministry concerns to your pastor and church staff. Sometimes referral will be needed. The ministry leader may be the communication link between the prospect or member and pastoral ministry.

The reaching, teaching, and witnessing in Sunday School does not occur in a vacuum. Members and prospects are real, hurting people. They may have brought hurt on themselves or be victims. Our response is to go beyond the walls of our comfort zones to extend help in Jesus' name.

10. MULTIPLY LEADERS AND UNITS.

We develop and implement an intentional process for continually multiplying leaders and new Bible study groups.

This best practice focuses on the need for an intentional, ongoing plan to multiply the leadership base and the number of teaching units. The word *multiply* is intentionally used instead of *add*. While both words suggest a numeric increase, to multiply suggests a more rapid and greater quantitative increase.

There is only one place to get teachers for preschool, children's, and student classes—from adult classes! Every teacher should establish a goal to discover and mentor one new teacher a year. The highest compliment any teacher can be paid is to be known for producing new teachers and encouraging members to seize opportunities to serve under God's call.

Starting new classes can be the most exciting work of your Sunday School, and can take place any time, especially when new units are clearly connected

to the vision. New units also can cause some of the greatest stress. A teacher in one church I served had the attitude "Many have tried, many have died! You won't take my people!" Her class was stagnant; outreach was nonexistent; ministry was limited to the few who attended. The class existed for the benefit of those who attended, not for the vision of the church.

Process for Multiplying Leaders and Units

Identify a target group. Although every believer is to be on mission to reach anyone and everyone, realistically each Bible study group needs to focus on a specific target group. The target group may develop around such factors as age, gender, marital status, life status, age of children, or transition points such as newly married, recently retired, recently widowed, and so forth.

Other target groups may consist of people who cannot or likely will not attend Bible study at the church on a Sunday morning. Such groups may include homebound adults and their caregivers; shift workers; employees who travel on weekends; residents of multihousing units; professionals who work on weekends, such as firefighters, police personnel, and hospital employees.

Because Sunday School as strategy is not defined by when or where it meets but by its purpose, consider creating Bible study groups that meet in nontraditional times and places. Examples include a home or office; a company conference room, a cafeteria break; a recreation site; or a residential institution.

Restructure existing classes or departments. Generally, a new unit should be started when an existing Bible study group reaches an enrollment or attendance that exceeds the number of persons who can be adequately cultivated and assimilated. A new group can be started by creating two or more groups from the existing group; for example, one fifth- and sixth-grade department can become one department for fifth graders, one for sixth graders.

Multiplication of classes can occur by enlisting specific attenders and targeting nonattenders. A new group can be created that focuses on the new target group. For example, one department may have three classes: coed ages 31-35, coed ages 36-42, and coed ages 43-49. Assigned classes are many men who do not attend but whose wives come. Several other men in these age ranges are church members but are not attending a Bible stud group.

To address those needs the department can be restructured to create a class for men and a class for women and to broaden the age groups of the coed classes. The new department would consist of these classes: coed ages 31-38 (because many women in this age group will attend the women's class), coed ages 39-49 (because several attenders agreed to be part of the men's or women's class), men ages 31-49, and women ages 31-49. A future class can at target new parents who would come from the coed class targeting ages 31-38.

No matter how the class or department is restructured, use terminology that

when naming classes

communicates the process in positive terms. Avoid using *split* or *divide*; instead, use words that communicate vision and intentionality.

Seek support. A successful new group needs a support system. Leaders need the encouragement that comes from knowing others are praying for them. Such support comes naturally when multiplication of leaders and units is part of an intentional strategy in which the leaders and the core of the new unit come from an existing class.

An existing class can help the new class discover, contact, and enroll prospects. Members from an existing class can work alongside one or more leaders in a new class. They might function as mentors, providing help in planning and teaching improvement, or serving as a FAITH Team Leader to team members from the new class.

One model often used successfully calls for the teacher of an existing class to mentor an apprentice for several months until that person is ready to take a class full-time. The teacher of the existing class begins a new class with seven or eight active members and the apprentice teacher becomes the leader of the original class. This approach seems to cause less distress on existing classes as the core group remains and only a few depart.

Enlist and build the leadership team. Those who help establish new work should be prepared to provide leadership in some way.

Promote the start date and location to the target group. Publicize the specific date, time, and place the new Bible study group will meet. Allow enough preparation time to communicate to the target group and other people affected. Invite potential members to a get-acquainted gathering in advance.

Invite and enroll members. Enrollment gives the Bible study group a tangible list of persons to whom they can minister and for whom they can pray.

Conduct the first session, with these elements:

Party—Provide time for fellowship, perhaps serving light snacks. Plan group-building and get-acquainted experiences.

Praise—Ask some leaders and members to tell how God is working in their lives. Read a psalm or other Scripture that will be part of the Bible study. Provide music. Be sensitive to the unchurched who are attending.

Prayer—Everyone has concerns for which they need God's intervention. Some new attenders may not be familiar with bringing concerns before God confident that He hears, understands, and answers.

Participation—Designate approximately two-thirds of the session for interactive Bible teaching.

[1]Michael D. Miller, *Kingdom Leadership* (Nashville: Convention Press, 1996), 72.
[2]Bob Horner, Ron Ralston, David Sunde, *The Promise Keeper at Work* (Nashville: Word Publishing, 1996), 111.

SECTION 3

How Vision and Curriculum Connect

When I was growing up in Alabama, my brothers, neighborhood friends, and I had great adventures in the thick woods behind our home. The acres of woods could hold our attention for hours at a time. This was where we would hunt for squirrels' nests, build forts out of discarded barn-roofing tin, climb trees that became lookout towers, chase dogs, pick buckets of fresh blackberries, and find the perfect Christmas tree.

The greatest of all adventures had to do with an old fallen tree deep in the woods. This was no ordinary tree. To the novice, it might appear to be a decaying great oak about 60 feet long and 10 feet around. But to 11-year-olds the tree came alive with imagination. One day it was a pirate ship where great battles took place; another day, a tightrope with tigers lurking underneath. At other times the tree was transformed into a rocket for a moon launch.

Next in importance to the tree was the path to get to it. Though located about a mile deep into the woods, we knew how to find it every time The path guided us to the tree, but the path was not simple; it was a secret passage-way. We had as much fun creating the path as we did playing on the tree.

First the path followed an old wagon lane so the uninformed would not notice the connection. Then it went through a thicket of briars, the first line of defense from would-be trackers. Next the path circled several different trees to confuse anyone who might stumble onto the path. Finally, the path took a secret final turn. A giant vine served as a swing to catapult us several yards over a gully and place us near our destination. When returning home, we kicked leaves to hide the trail.

Over time a well-worn dirt path emerged. Many tennis shoes, one step at a time, created this path. Much of that path is still visible 40 years later. In recent years I retraced this journey with my own boys, showing them the crazy path only 11-year-old boys with carefree summer days can dream up.

I am sure I take for granted the experiences I had as a child with the great tree in the woods. But I know one thing: paths are worn from relationships and tell life stories. A well-worn path takes time to emerge. A path is a reflection of what is significant or important in life because the same continuous interactions occur over and over again.

We create spiritual paths too. Spiritual paths are worn from one's relationship with God. A well-worn spiritual path takes time, a lifetime if you will, to emerge. Such a path is a reflection of what is significant in life because continuous interactions with God happen over and over to create the path.

The Scriptures often use the imagery of a path to describe our spiritual journey. David penned many songs in Psalms that came out of personal experience, notably Psalm 23:3 and Psalm 25:4-5. In Psalm 27:11, David cried out for God to "Teach me your way, O Lord; Lead me in a straight path . . . ." Similarly, the writer of Proverbs 3:5-6 called for the followers of God to "Trust in the Lord with all your heart and lean not on your own understanding; in all your ways acknowledge him, and he will make your paths straight."

Making a Personal Connection

What do you think your life will be like 20 years from now? What spiritual difference do you think you will make with your life? If you are married, do you hope to have children? Be a grandparent? Be fully engaged in your career? Enjoying retirement? In the following spaces, describe your desired level of spiritual maturity in the 2020s:

untempted

One word God might use to describe the spiritual path you hope to achieve.

dangerous edge

Two adjectives describing your spiritual condition today.

Pray   Heal   do

Three verbs identifying new spiritual steps you would like to start or improve.

Effective   Godly   Kingdom   ldr

A four-word thought about your future spiritual goal.

Connecting Sunday School to Life

Taking the Right Path

As you think about your life, your church, your family, your community, and our society as a whole; would it not be fair to say that, a few years past the turn of the century, our churches are standing at a crossroads? What difference can a teacher of the Word of God make in the fabric of people's lives?

The prophet Jeremiah faced a remarkably similar situation. Jeremiah came of age during the closing years of the seventh century B.C. He was both a witness to the fall of Assyrian domination and a prophet of the rise of Babylonian power. Pagan religious practices had become common among the people of God. Altars to Baal were erected. The people turned to sorcery and witchcraft and worshiped the stars. Many of the religious priests were wicked. The people of God, for the most part, had forsaken God.

Jeremiah probably was only an older teenager or a young adult when "the word of the Lord came to him" (Jer. 1:2) to warn the people to change their ways or God's judgment would prevail. But in the midst of the stern warning in Jeremiah 6, God showed the people how they could avoid destruction: "This is what the Lord says: 'Stand at the crossroads and look; ask for the ancient paths, ask where the good way is, and walk in it, and you will find rest for your souls'" (v. 16).

Jeremiah described the people of God as being at a crossroads. He identified four actions they could take to find the way God approves: "stand . . . look; . . . ask, . . . walk." These verbs can be applied to the actions spiritual leaders—teachers of God's Word—can take to point people to God's path.

Stand—The Hebrew verb is the same one God said to Moses at the burning bush (Ex. 3:5, NIV): "The place where you are standing is holy ground"; the same word used of God at the tabernacle (Ex. 33:10, NIV): "Whenever the people saw the pillar of cloud standing at the entrance of the tent, they all stood and worshiped"; the same word used in Proverbs 12:7, NIV: "Wicked men are overthrown and are no more, but the house of the righteous stands firm." The verb means "to stand still" or "to stand fast." The Christian teacher is to pause, stop, halt during the course of living, and evaluate the direction of life.

Look—The Hebrew verb is the same one used in Genesis 1:4: "God saw that the light was good"; the same word Moses used with the children of Israel when they were hungry (Ex. 16:7): "In the morning you will see the glory of the Lord"; the same word used by Isaiah to describe his vision of God (Isa. 6:1): "I saw the Lord seated on a throne, high and exalted." The verb means "to see, to behold, and to consider." To look and to see is to become aware and, therefore, accountable. The Christian teacher is to peer down the crossroads to consider the consequences of the path that leads to death and the consequences of the path that leads to life.

Ask—Jeremiah instructed the people to ask or to inquire. They could choose to follow God's way—the ancient path of holiness, obedience, and love—or they could continue down the road they had chosen toward certain death. In this context, asking implies listening to God's instructions and following Him. The Christian teacher is to ask of God, listen to Him, and rely on His strength to follow His way.

Walk—The Hebrew verb is the same one used in Psalm 23:4: "Even though I walk through the valley of the shadow of death, I will fear no evil"; the same word used in the classic Deuteronomy 6:6-7 passage. The verb means "to go on" or, in today's vernacular, to "walk the talk." The Christian teacher is to walk the good way, demonstrating Christian integrity and character, and to grow in Christian discipleship.

The chosen but rebellious people of God failed to stand, look, ask, and walk in the way of the Lord. The Kingdom of Judah was overthrown by Babylon in 587 B.C. and the temple was destroyed. The people chose the wrong path. Only a remnant of faithful followers of God remained.

The spiritual condition of today's world mirrors that of Jeremiah's day. The following trends provide evidence that the way Christians think and live is not significantly different from that of non-Christians:

1. A secular, postmodern society has emerged permeated by a "truth-is-relative" philosophy.
2. Alternate belief systems within a tolerant, pluralistic culture compete with the absolute truth of biblical Christianity.
3. The state of many Christian families continues to lack a moral and spiritual foundation and direction.
4. The rise of the "every other Sunday" churchgoer indicates a low level of commitment.
5. Many Christian believers ignore or deny biblical authority and obedience to God.
6. The absence or decline of intentional personal evangelism underscores believers' indifference in sharing their faith.
7. A startling level of biblical illiteracy exists among Christians, especially among the youngest generations.
8. Laypersons in the church are increasingly incapable of expressing a Christian doctrinal apologetic or basic biblical beliefs they can share with non-Christians.
9. The overreliance on secular models of education, especially the humanistic influence of "meeting felt needs," overshadows Jesus' call for self-sacrifice and service.
10. Christians give an estimated 5 percent of their weekly time to spiritual activity.

Connecting Sunday School to Life

As civilization catapults through the third millennium A.D., the Christian world is in need of a spiritual turning point that compels Christians to adhere to biblical authority, to affirm absolute truth, and to integrate a biblical worldview into their lives.

Making a Personal Connection: Reflect on Your Journey
Have you reached a crossroad in your spiritual journey? Consider what you must do today to ensure ongoing vitality in your Christian walk.

In what way do you need to "stand" or evaluate your spiritual life?

Do you need to "look" down the crossroads and view the consequences of your actions?

What do you need to "ask" of God?

How could you improve the way you "walk" with God?

Influencing the Spiritual Paths of Learners
Have you ever taken a good look around your church and thought about the hundreds, perhaps thousands, of people who have created paths through your church? What became of them? Did they become something different because of their experiences in the church?

Did a first-time visitor come back for a second look? Was a baby greeted with a warm smile and sung a song about Jesus? Was a teenager challenged to think about his or her relationship with God? Did adults engage in Bible study that caused them to change their behavior?

I teach third graders at Brentwood Baptist Church in Brentwood, Tennessee. Sometimes it is a stretch for me to connect with eight-year-olds! They have so many basic questions, are so full of energy, and have such interesting perspectives about life. I know that responses from teachers typically have a profound spiritual effect on them. I work with third graders because I know what a significant period of time it is for a child to learn about God.

Recently my church moved into a new building, and the church had an open house. I began to wonder about the children I had come to know over the past year who would walk down the long hallway, begin to make a path though this room, and go out again into the routine of their daily lives.

On that day Matthew had never entered this room to be taught the Bible. Crystal, a soon-to-be visitor, had yet to hesitantly poke her head in to see what was happening. No Scripture verse had been read aloud by Benjamin, no question about Jesus asked by Elizabeth.

What would become of the children who would make a spiritual path through this room each week? What kind of biblical foundation would they develop to move them on to their next paths as older children, as teenagers, and then as young adults?

Spiritual transformation through biblical learning is a continuous, lifelong process. Spiritual transformation is God's work of changing a believer into the likeness of Jesus by creating a new identity in Christ and by empowering a lifelong relationship of love, trust, and obedience to glorify God.

Every Sunday School teacher teaches in the name of God and by His authority guides learners in God's truth. A teacher is an instrument used of God as an agent of spiritual transformation. God works through teachers to point people toward a path, a way of life in relationship with God. Teachers, like the psalmist, call upon God to "guide me in your truth and teach me" (Ps. 25:5).

Using Sunday School to Build the Path

Bible study groups that are designed primarily for reaching lost people are open groups. The best curriculum is designed around this premise.

Designing a Bible Study Curriculum Path

One way to view curriculum is as the "the continuous path, course, process, or system for open Bible study groups to lay foundations for children, to guide unbelievers toward faith in Christ, and to guide believers toward Christlikeness integrating biblical truth into the learner's life." If Sunday School is the foundational strategy in a local church for leading people to faith in the Lord Jesus Christ and for building on-mission Christians through open Bible study groups that engage people in evangelism, discipleship, ministry, fellowship, and worship, how would you design a curriculum to carry out this strategy?

Making a Personal Connection: Where Would You Start?

If you could design a Bible study curriculum plan for your church, where would you start? Based on the definitions of curriculum and Sunday School, what principles would you establish for building an effective curriculum plan?

Connecting Sunday School to Life

View the streaming video (**CD-ROM**) and consider these features; they will become our focus for the remainder of this section.

1. Preparing faithfully for the open group Bible teaching session, including personal spiritual preparation and participation in leadership meetings.
2. Encountering God's Word in a Bible study group that guides learners toward spiritual transformation.
3. Continuing to guide learners toward spiritual transformation in daily living and family relationships.
4. Centering the transformational teaching-learning process around key Bible teaching elements.
5. Preparing open group lesson plans with variety, including relational, musical, logical, physical, reflective, visual, and verbal approaches.
6. Looking for opportunities in other settings to teach and model the message of the Bible.
7. Equipping parents to be the primary Bible teachers in their homes.
8. Choosing open group Bible study materials that lead learners to explore the entire counsel of God during their life stages.
9. Providing the best possible teaching resources that enable teachers to teach for spiritual transformation.
10. Providing the best possible age-appropriate space and equipment.

Understanding the Path That Starts and Ends at Home

Sunday School as strategy is built on the biblical assertion of training and instruction through the eternal partnership of church and family. In the New Testament the Greek word for training as found in 2 Timothy 3:16 and Ephesians 6:4, *paideia*, means a blend of instruction, discipline, and personal guidance. Generally, instruction means "to train or direct learners to build their lives upon a structure of authoritative precepts or truths." Instruction has "edge" to it, in that those who instruct have a sense of urgency, passion, and seriousness about their task. This concept of instruction reflects the heart-beat of the Bible (Ps. 32:8; 119:133; Prov. 16:20; Rom. 15:14).

Moses instructed a new generation, who were on the brink of entering the promised land, to remember the mighty acts of God and to obey God's way of life. He called on the nation of Israel to love God (Deut. 6:4-6). Moses appealed to the people of Israel and especially parents to teach their children to observe and to obey all that he had taught them about God's ways.

Jesus called on a new generation of leaders—also on the brink, this time of spreading the gospel around the world—to make disciples of all nations. In short, He called them to Great Commission work and to become Great Commission Christians. God commands people to love Him completely and to love others. God loves all people and desires that they hear the gospel and receive salvation through His Son (John 3:16; Rom. 1:16-17; 2 Pet. 3:9).

Sunday School recognizes God's active purpose of reconciling a spiritually lost world to Himself and provides a way for people to join Him in the work of intentional evangelism. Sunday School leads people to faith in the Lord Jesus Christ. "Christ Commission work" requires evangelism—Christian believers sharing the gospel with spiritually lost people.

Instruction through the home in partnership with the church is the primary biblical model by which the Holy Spirit transforms lives (Prov. 22:6; Eph. 6:4; 2 Tim. 1:5-7). God desires for parents to teach His Word to their children as an integral and natural part of daily living.

Parents should be equipping their children to learn how to study and integrate God's Word into their lives. Within the context of the home, parents can teach the Christian worldview to their children, who are bombarded with many cultural worldviews. Anytime a parent learns a new truth from God's Word in worship, Sunday School, or personal Bible study, he or she should ask, "How can I help my child in time to understand, live, and obey this truth I have just learned?"

Teaching That Transforms

Every Sunday School teacher desires to see the lives of learners transformed. Consider these basic principles for teaching to transforms lives:
1. Christian teaching is a divine calling, a spiritual gift, and a ministry.
2. Christian teaching is motivated by teachers' love of God and love of others to guide them in the study of His Word.
3. Christian teaching trusts the Holy Spirit to work and to transform people through the learning process.
4. Christian teaching means learning sound methods of biblical interpretation.
5. Christian teaching depends on a teacher's own personal spiritual growth and relationship with God.
6. Christian teaching uses a variety of learning techniques that match learning styles and cause the learner to interact with the Scriptures.
7. Christian teaching uses Bible study curriculum resources as tools to enhance the learning experience.
8. Christian teaching provides a learning environment that encourages trust, openness, and the sharing of concerns, needs, and praises.
9. Christian teaching challenges learners to apply biblical truth to their lives.
10. Christian teaching is a process that happens wherever the teacher goes as others observe the teacher's character and conduct in real-life situations.

Three key words express the basic design for teaching and learning in preschool through adult curriculum: *Prepare, Encounter,* and *Continue*. To begin, leaders prepare not only a lesson but also themselves. Then leaders and

Connecting Sunday School to Life

learners encounter God's Word in the context of a Bible study group as together they acknowledge the authority of Who is in charge of their lives, search the biblical truth, discover the truth, and personalize the truth. They then struggle with the truth and decide whether to believe and obey the truth as they continue to live and learn in daily relationships, especially with families.

Sunday School teachers should not assume that all participants have completed preparation before the session. Instead, Sunday morning leaders must plan to introduce participants to biblical truth that can transform their lives during and after the session. Leaders can help participants continue to focus on the truth after the session through learner guides, devotional guides, and personal and family relationships. Participants will also have the opportunity to reinforce the truth the following Sunday.

Practically speaking, how do teachers prepare, encounter, and continue their work? (Also see age-group e-books on the **CD-ROM**.)

First, before the session, prepare (2 Tim. 2:15). Effective Sunday School teachers do not just prepare lessons; they allow God to prepare them. People will long remember the character of the leader more than the content of the lesson (Phil. 4:9). Key principles of learning emerge for teachers to build into each teaching-learning experience.

1. Learning happens best when teachers recognize that every person is a unique individual created by God with different needs, skills, gifts, interests, and abilities.
2. Learning happens best when learning is approached as a lifelong process directly related to the learner's dimension of the spiritual life.
3. Learning happens best in response to Bible study that is relevant and relates to personal needs and interests.
4. Learning happens best when individuals are active and involved rather than passive and nonparticipatory.
5. Learning happens best when the Bible study experience takes into account learners' generational worldview.
6. Learning happens best when learners interact in a learning environment where they sense genuine care, belonging, and a climate of trust.
7. Learning happens best in small groups where learners have the opportunity to build trusting relationships, share their spiritual journeys, and interact with the living Word of God for personal application.
8. Learning happens best when learners use multiple senses in the learning experience.
9. Learning happens best when learners are motivated by the Holy Spirit to become responsible for their own learning.
10. Learning happens best when learners see evidence of personal spiritual growth in their daily lives.

If preparing to teach is the first major step, then what is the best way for teachers to prepare? There are two broad ways:

1. Through the leadership meeting, in which leaders pray and focus on the mission of the Sunday School/church, focus on relationships, and focus on Bible study.
2. Through personal Bible study, in which leaders prepare personally for God to use them to teach His Word and prepare for learners to encounter God's Word. Effective leaders depend on the Holy Spirit for He is already at work in the lives of participants.

The Biblical Process of Instruction

Understanding how God uses His Word to transform lives is critical to personal Bible study preparation and developing a lesson plan. Your LifeWay Sunday School Bible study resources are designed to engage both leaders and learners in the biblical process of instruction that leads to spiritual transformation.

This transformational teaching-learning process features seven Bible teaching elements—common concepts for all age groups. For the Holy Spirit to transform lives, participants must experience all elements before, during, and/or after the session. While some people may need these elements in sequenced steps, others may prefer a different sequence or repetition throughout the session or unit. Spiritual transformation will occur over a period of time from several lessons in a unit to a lifetime, as foundations are laid in younger years for spiritual conversion and transformation.

As leaders plan their Bible study, they should reflect on how God is changing them into the likeness of Jesus by asking these questions:

- Acknowledge authority: Who or what authority *controls* my life?
- Search the Scripture: What historical setting and key words are reflected in the *content* of this Bible text?
- Discover the truth: What eternal *concept* is the Holy Spirit revealing to me from this Scripture?
- Personalize the truth: In my life *context* what is God teaching me personally from this Scripture?
- Struggle with the truth: What *conflict* or crisis of belief is the Holy Spirit bringing about in my heart and life?
- Believe the truth: What new biblical *conviction* is God leading me to integrate into my life?
- Obey the truth: How is the Holy Spirit changing my *conduct* in how I think, what I value, and the way I live?

Now look at how these seven Bible teaching elements find expression in a good teaching plan for use during and after the session.

Second, during the session, encounter (2 Tim. 3:16-17). Every good Bible study session will have a flow to it. From the moment people arrive, activities

Connecting Sunday School to Life

must grab their attention. Every participant comes to a Bible teaching session with an authority—recognized or unrecognized—that controls his or her life ("acknowledge authority"). Leaders recognize that they are engaged in spiritual warfare for every person's mind. The beginning of the teaching plan, then, attempts to focus every individual's heart toward learning biblical truth that connects with his or her life.

Usually, the next part of the teaching plan engages people in searching the Scriptures for biblical content and concepts they can understand for life today ("search the truth [Scripture])" and "discover the truth"). The key word *content* typically focuses on the question, What does the Bible passage say? This first question is the most crucial one, and involves examining the meaning of words and phrases of the Bible content with careful attention. For the majority of teachers, this means using sound and reliable translations of the Bible.

Begin with identifying what the text says to you. Initially avoid reviewing comments from other writers. Read the passage of Scripture several times. Identify key words and phrases. Outlining the passage can be helpful. Summarize and reflect on what God was saying to the original readers, and allow God to speak and connect with you through His living Word. Consider these factors as you read the Bible text:

The linguistic factor—This element deals with the intended meaning of words and phrases, the relationship of words, and the kind of literature in a particular part of the Scriptures. Is the text from the law? poetry? Was the text originally a letter? Build a library of basic Bible study resources including a Bible concordance, Bible dictionary, Bible atlas, and Bible commentaries.

The historical factor—When studying a text of Scripture, identify the historical setting. The historical setting and customs usually provides insights that help the reader understand and enrich the meaning of the text itself.

The holistic factor—This element focuses on the place of the text in the Bible as a whole. What do other passages in the Bible say about this topic or issue? If the author of the book has written other books in the Bible, what light do these books shed on the passage? The holistic factor helps avoid proof-texting, or pulling a passage out of the Scripture and using it to mean whatever one chooses to make it mean.

The word *concept* focuses on this question: What is the meaning of the biblical truth from the Bible passage? Learning to discover biblical truth is a crucial goal of Bible study. Studying the words and phases, the historical setting, and other dimensions of the content prepares the learner to get to the heart of Bible study—the biblical concept or truth or principle that God is trying to teach the Christian. Being open to the leadership of the Holy Spirit can equip teachers to identify and guide learners to explore the abiding truths of Scripture.

Teaching plans, however, also must move people to "personalize the

truth." The key word *context* focuses on, How does the meaning of the biblical truth relate to the learner's life context? At this juncture in the Bible study process, the teacher's level of understanding the life context and needs of learners plays a critical role. Ten life markers can serve as helpful categories for identifying the needs of learners:

- What is their biblical worldview?
- What is their generational worldview?
- What is their educational level and preferred learning style?
- What is their age and life stage?
- What gender issues impact them?
- What race and ethnicity issues impact them?
- What is their lifestyle affinity (single, married, divorced, widowed)?
- What are their personality characteristics?
- What region and community distinctives might impact them?
- What socioeconomic or career issues do they face?

The teacher needs to ask these questions about each learner's life context: From which dimension of the spiritual life will the learner view the Bible text? If the learner is lost, how can the truth be understood from his or her point of view? What specific generational issues does he or she face? What is the learning style of each member and which teaching strategy will be most effective?

Specific, relevant, personal life application of biblical truth grows out of the teacher's ability to customize application to the needs of the learners. Customization happens as the Holy Spirit guides the teacher to recognize and be sensitive to the spiritual needs of the learners.

After a learner struggles with the truth and after the learner comes to believe the truth, the final key word, *conduct*, focuses on answering, What changes in personal conduct should result from applying the biblical truth?

This final element of creating effective Bible study is perhaps the most difficult but rewarding for both the teacher and the learner. At this stage, if the learner has been open to the Holy Spirit's leadership, he or she is confronted with a change that needs to be made in order to become more Christlike. The learner should consider these issues:

- What command did God present?
- What promise did God teach, and how do I claim it?
- What truth should I believe from this passage?
- What attitudes or values need changing in my life?
- What actions or behaviors need changing in my life?
- What sin is God convicting me to confess?
- Am I obeying God's Word as taught in this passage?
- Is God leading me to minister to someone?
- Is God leading me to witness to someone?

Connecting Sunday School to Life

Inevitably, people will experience inner conflict as biblical truth intersects with their personal life ("struggle with the truth"). Application is not complete until this conflict is resolved by change of belief, attitude, and action as reflected in a lifestyle of love, trust, and obedience that glorifies God ("believe the truth" and "obey the truth"). This almost always comes after the session.

Third, after the session, continue (Col. 2:6-7). Because teaching doesn't stop when the session concludes, teachers continue their teaching ministry 24 hours a day, 7 days a week. Teachers may enlist class or department members as leaders to help continue the teaching-learning ministry. Here are some tips:

1. Practice a daily quiet time of reading the Bible. LifeWay Sunday School devotional guides and selected learner guides have devotionals that relate to Sunday School lessons in Family Bible Study.
2. Pray by name for the individuals and families represented in your class.
3. Contact at least one person on roll each week. You could see them at their home, school, job, or anywhere. You could call or write them (email, too!). Ask questions such as:
   - (To those who were present) How has our last Bible study helped you or your family this week? (To those who were absent) Here's what we are talking about in this week's Bible study.
   - How is your family? (Ask for permission to report any crisis to your church.)
   - (In a spirit of humility to those who haven't come in a long time) How have we at the church or Sunday School let you down? How can we pray for you and your family?
   - May I tell you the greatest thing that has happened to me? In your personal opinion, what do you understand it takes for a person to go to heaven? (Then share your testimony and/or the plan of salvation from the learner guide or devotional guide.)
4. Visit, call, write, or contact prospects. Take a learner guide and/or devotional guide. Offer to show them the plan of salvation or features that relate to the week's Bible study.
5. Help plan fellowship or ministry events with your class or department.

Finally, effective Sunday School leaders hold themselves as well as their learners accountable for obeying what God teaches from Sunday to Sunday. Every Bible study participant expects the teacher to come prepared to teach, for every leader is the lesson in the sense of being accountable to live what the Bible teaches (1 Thess. 1:6-7). What if participants came prepared to report on what God taught them or how God had used them in ministry since the previous Bible study session? What if they brought someone who needed to hear God's Word? Talk about teaching that transforms lives 24-7!

Making a Personal Connection: Practice the Elements

Practice using the elements for effective Bible study and create a basic Bible study lesson plan. Using a separate sheet of paper, complete the following steps based on John 4:1-42. Use only your Bible. Refer to the explanations of the elements as needed. Consider the members of your class for applications.

1. **Content: What does the Bible passage say?** Read the passage, identify key words, make a brief outline, summarize the text.
2. **Concept: What is the meaning of the biblical truth from the Bible passage?** Do you view your role as a teacher more like a potter or more like a gardener? What truths did you discover, and what key questions could you use in class?
3. **Context: How does the meaning of the biblical truth relate to the learner's life context?** Using the 10 life markers, what issues relate to this study?
4. **Conduct: What changes in personal conduct should result from applying the biblical truth?** (descriptive sentence)

What is the value of completing this approach to Bible study? What limitations did you discover from using this Bible study approach?

Establishing a Lifelong Path for Bible Learning

Curriculum Characteristics

One of the key best practices for an effective Sunday School is to teach to transform. Sunday School emphasizes ongoing, open Bible study groups that reproduce new groups as the best long-term approach for building a ministry environment that guides preschoolers and children toward conversion through foundational teaching, that encourages unsaved people to come to faith in Christ, that assimilates new believers into the life of the church, and that encourages believers to lead others to Christ. Sunday School leaders need to map out sound, open group Bible study curriculum that causes learners to explore the whole counsel of God during the life stages of the learners.

Curriculum is the continuous course, process, or system for Bible study groups to lay foundations for children, to guide unbelievers toward faith in Christ, and to guide believers toward Christlikeness integrating biblical truth into the life. All LifeWay Bible study resources emphasize the following 10 characteristics. (See the **CD-ROM** for details of these characteristics.)

- Biblical authority
- The kingdom of God
- The biblical worldview
- Sunday School strategy
- Foundational evangelism
- Foundational discipleship

Connecting Sunday School to Life

- Family responsibility
- Spiritual transformation
- Biblical leadership
- Teaching that transforms lives

Learning Approaches

The teacher has the strategic role of selecting ways to communicate the Bible message that reflect knowledge of the learners, their varied approaches to learning, and their levels of understanding. All Bible studies provide a wide variety of interactive, age-appropriate learning activities including:

- *Relational:* activities that focus on interaction and cooperation with others.
- *Musical:* activities that focus on music, singing, and performing.
- *Logical:* activities that focus on problem-solving such as puzzles or debates.
- *Natural:* activities that focus on exploring elements in the natural world.
- *Physical:* activities that focus on active involvement in projects and skills.
- *Reflective:* activities that focus on self-expression.
- *Visual:* activities that focus on visual images.
- *Verbal:* activities that focus on reading, writing, speaking, and listening.

Distinctives of Family Bible Study ★

Bible study approach—Family Bible Study reflects a common curriculum plan designed to achieve the goal of building the family of faith to live by God's truth. This Bible study plan provides a common Bible study theme each week for the five Sunday School age divisions—preschool, children, youth, young adults, and adults—with common Bible passages for all ages as often as suitable and balanced with age-group distinctives. This study plan encourages Bible study at home through Family Bible Time, a weekly emphasis for parents to guide their children in a discussion of the Bible study theme.

Bible translation—Family Bible Study offers Bible translation editions in the King James Version (KJV) for adults in the nongraded resources and for youth in the broadly graded resources. The Holman Christian Standard Bible text is used in all closely graded resources for adults, youth, and children and also is available in nongraded resources for adults and in broadly graded resources for youth. Preschool resources are usable with any Bible translation. Broadly graded children's resources work equally well with either the Holman Christian Standard Bible or the King James Version. The Scripture text is printed in youth learner guides and in all adult age-group materials. Children's memory verses are printed in both New International Version (NIV) and KJV in the broadly graded resources and in NIV in the closely graded resources.

Bible study plan—Family Bible Study uses a comprehensive, balanced, and appropriately sequenced study of Bible books, people, doctrine, history, and classic Bible passages. The content is organized around biblical worldview categories and addresses life issues. The common Bible study theme provides an opportunity to reinforce the biblical message during the Sunday experience through Bible teaching and through music and the pastor's sermon.

Target audiences—Churches: Closely graded and broadly graded editions enable churches of all sizes to address distinctive age-group and generational life needs as appropriate to their unique situations. Families—Common Bible study themes and other features provide parents and other family members unique opportunities for continuing Bible study and application.

Bible instruction—Family Bible Study instructional design and Bible study resources assume the learners do not complete advanced preparation before the session, except for senior adults and groups that target broad age spans of adults. Instead, each new lesson theme is introduced on Sunday. Learners are guided to engage in studying the Bible text during the session. Learners continue to focus on the theme during the week using learner guides and devotional resources. All leader guides provide a 60-minute teaching plan and reflect a common lesson format using *Prepare, Encounter*, and *Continue* segments.

Publishing cycle—Family Bible Study resources are published dated and released quarterly for the four seasons: Fall (September-November), Winter (December-February), Spring (March-May), and Summer (June-August).

Bible study resources—A wide range of economically priced materials is provided including learner guides, leader guides, leader packs (some with CD-ROMs) for both closely graded and broadly graded organizational patterns as well as options for Bible translation in the KJV and in the HCSB. Interactive learner guides are designed as tools for parents and teachers to engage learners in a meaningful and life-transforming study of God's Word.

EXTRA! electronic teaching plan supplements are provided weekly by Internet (LifeWay.com). Supplemental Family Bible Study resources also are available for all age-group leaders. The *Biblical Illustrator* features additional Bible background and color photography and graphics on people, places, and events in the Bible study. *Advanced Bible Study Commentary* and *The Herschel Hobbs Commentary* provide additional Bible background helps for all age-group teachers and adult learners using Family Bible Study.

Family Bible devotions—Supportive resources include devotions that relate to the weekly common Bible study theme. Resources include *More, Adventure, Bible Express, essential connection (ec),* and *Open Windows* (regular, large-print, and audiocassette editions). Devotional elements are included in selected adult learner guides and in all preschool learner guides.

Spanish edition—A Spanish language edition of Family Bible Study is available for preschool, children, adults/youth including leader guides, learner guides, and leader packs. The curriculum study plan follows the English Family Bible Study but is delayed one year to allow for translation. A supportive Spanish devotional resource for adults, *Quietud*, follows the *Open Windows* devotional plan, also delayed one year.

Distinctives of Explore the Bible Series (Adults) ✦

Bible study approach—Explore the Bible Series provides a systematic approach to all the books of the Bible in ways appropriate to the needs of adults.

Bible translation—Explore the Bible Series is based on Holman Christian Standard Bible. Some periodicals print both the HCSB and the KJV. The Scripture text is printed in the materials.

Bible study plan—This Bible study plan covers all 66 Bible books and is based on the nature, structure, and content of the Bible as a whole and of Bible books.

Target audience—Explore the Bible Series is designed for adults in churches of all sizes who desire book studies covering all the books of the Bible using a curriculum plan driven by Bible structure.

Bible instruction—Explore the Bible Series instructional design and Bible study resources assume the learners complete advanced preparation before the session. Learners are guided to engage in study of the Bible text before and during the session.

Publishing cycle—Explore the Bible Series resources are published dated and released quarterly for the four seasons: Fall, Winter, Spring, and Summer.

Bible study resources—Economically priced materials are provided including learner guides, leader guides, and leader packs. Supplemental resources are available for further preparation or advanced study by learners. EXTRA! electronic teaching plan supplements are provided weekly LifeWay.com.

Devotional guide resources—Separate devotionals for adults are found in *Open Windows* (regular, large-print, and audiocassette editions), *Journey* (for women), and *Stand Firm* (for men).

Language editions—Explore the Bible Series also features language editions in Korean and Chinese translated from the English materials and based on the same curriculum cycle. Vietnamese resources, as well as materials for the deaf, are provided with original writing based on the curriculum cycle. Only a Korean learner guide is provided. Teaching helps are included in the learner guides of Chinese, Vietnamese, and deaf materials.

Distinctives of LifeTrak (Younger and Older Youth) ✦

Bible study approach—LifeTrak curriculum is an undated set of 13 Bible studies released quarterly that use a topic-driven Bible study plan.

Bible translation—LifeTrak is based on the Holman Christian Standard Bible. The Bible text is not printed.

Bible study plan—This Bible study plan covers the message of the Bible and is organized around current developmental life issues distinctive to younger youth and older youth.

Target audience—LifeTrak is designed for churches who want undated Bible study resources with distinctive curriculum plans for younger and older youth.

Bible instruction—LifeTrak instructional design and Bible study resources assume the learners do not complete advanced preparation before the session. Instead, each new Bible study is introduced in the session. Learners are guided to engage in study of the Bible text during the session using in-class reproducible take-home student sheets and an occasional parent newsletter to enhance family involvement with their youth in the study.

All sessions provide a 60-minute teaching plan and reflect the common lesson format using *Prepare, Encounter*, and *Continue* and the seven Bible teaching-learning elements.

Publishing cycle—LifeTrak resources are released quarterly and contain 13 undated sessions that can be used in sequence or in any order you choose.

Bible study resources—LifeTrak curriculum includes an all-in-one leader guide for younger youth and an all-in-one leader guide for older youth. Both contain everything teachers need to organize and implement an effective Bible study ministry for one Youth Sunday School class, including reproducible student and parent pages and a CD-ROM.

Devotional guide resource—Separate devotionals for youth are found in *essential connection* (ec).

Distinctives of *Essentials for Life After High School* (12th Graders) ★
Bible study approach—Essentials is a set of 13 Bible studies to help high school seniors find biblical guidance to prepare for life after high school.

Bible translation—Essentials is based on the Holman Christian Standard Bible. The Bible text is not printed.

Bible study plan—This Bible study plan is based on distinctive life concerns of 12th-grade students.

Target audience—Essentials is designed for churches that want a quarter of Bible studies to help prepare 12th-grade students for life beyond high school.

Bible instruction—*Essentials for Life After High School* instructional design and Bible study resources assume the learners do not complete advanced preparation before the session. Instead, each new lesson theme is introduced in the session. Learners are guided to engage in study of the Bible text during the session using their own learner guide, continuing to focus on the Bible study to integrate the truth into their lives after the session.

In the leader guide all sessions provide a 60-minute teaching plan that is

# Connecting Sunday School to Life

supplemented with multimedia presentations. Students also can study the learner guide on their own if their church does not have a group study.

Bible study resources—Materials include a learner guide and a leader guide.

Devotional guide resource—Separate devotionals for youth are found in *essential connection (ec)*.

Distinctives of *Everything You Need to Know to Be a Teenager* ☆
Bible study approach—This Bible study plan is designed to help sixth graders discover what the Bible says, demonstrate their understanding of what they learn, and be discipled in their relationship with Christ.

Bible translation—The Bible text is not printed. Children's memory verses are printed.

Bible study plan—The Bible study plan is designed to help sixth graders look at Baptist beliefs, make choices based on biblical principles, and build Christian character into their lives. Content is based on Bible passages related to the doctrine of humanity, salvation, evangelism, God, and the Bible. Each unit on Christian characteristics is based on the life of a biblical person.

Target audience—*Everything You Need to Know to Be a Teenager* is designed for churches that want undated Bible study resources with distinctive curriculum plans for sixth-grade students.

Bible instruction—The instructional design is built around three elements: **Dig** gets sixth graders into Bible study. They study Bible word meaning, compare Bible translations, paraphrase Bible stories, or complete verse-by-verse studies of Bible passages. **Discuss and Do** help sixth graders talk about biblical principles and begin to relate them to real-life issues. **Decide** gives sixth graders an opportunity to practice biblical principles in a safe, nonthreatening atmosphere. This design enables sixth graders to think carefully about the choices they make now and about those they will face in the future.

Bible study resources—Each of four quarterly sets of *Everything You Need to Know to be a Teenager* undated resources is unique and consists of a leader guide, a learner guide, and a resource box filled with teaching helps and a video designed to focus the learning.

Devotional guide resource—Separate devotionals for sixth graders are found in *Bible Express*.

Undated Resources Provide Bible Study Options

A vibrant experience with supporting resources for children, called *G-Force,* involves children grades 1-6 in music, interactive games, Bible study, and personal application. As soon as kids enter the room, they are involved in interactive activities. They move to music, in which they learn the session's main point and memory verse. Boys and girls then transition to small groups

for personal application. Supporting resources include a leader guide, cards, a visual pack, a training video, a CD-ROM/DVD, and a family CD-ROM. G-Force can be used during the Bible study time, in a combined Sunday School-worship schedule, or on Wednesday or Sunday evenings.

Two options open possibilities for reaching and teaching adults. Described as a community-building resource, *Life Connections* offers seven undated studies to help build relationships in context of Bible study. *Life Connections* is designed for small groups as well as master teacher-type groups that want to strengthen fellowship. This line is an excellent choice for seeker-oriented individuals or new believers.

MasterWork: Essential Messages from His Servants offers in-depth Bible studies featuring key messages from well-known authors. *MasterWork* is available quarterly for ongoing Bible study groups that want to use dated materials.

For ongoing information about new resources, check your dated ordering materials and LifeWay.com for complete details.

Discovering the Benefits of Using LifeWay Sunday School Resources
The study of God's Word can be enhanced by resources that recognize the value of Bible study and that support a ministry strategy that is achieved through an open Bible study group. LifeWay Sunday School curriculum resources provide churches with certain key benefits (**CD-ROM** item "Benefits of Using LifeWay Sunday School Resources").

Understanding Key Elements in Biblical Studies Design for an Open Group
At best, the average Christian adult spends about 5 percent of his or her time in spiritual activities in the course of a week. These activities, both home and church, include Bible study preparation and interaction in small-group experiences. On the other hand, the average adult spends 20 percent of his week's time watching television, listening to the radio, or other discretionary media-based activities. Time for Bible study competes in a world of intense activities. An adult who maintains an active church life has the opportunity for thousands of Bible study classes over a lifetime.

Churches, Bible study leaders, and individuals want to make the best use of Bible study times. How does a church or class go about guiding the Bible study experiences that cause adults to be exposed to the whole truth of God? What is the best way to arrange and blend topical studies that focus on relevant adult needs and issues and Bible book studies that focus on truths in that book? How should studies from both Old and New Testaments be incorporated? How often should Christians study the life of Christ? What Scriptures could be studied by a person in the "lost" dimension that would help them understand how to become a Christian? When should Christian doctrines and disciplines be studied? When should an evangelistic emphasis be stressed in the class?

Connecting Sunday School to Life

These significant questions lift up the value of developing a sound Bible study curriculum plan. A sound plan features three significant characteristics:

1. Comprehensiveness—This aspect of a curriculum plan includes everything essential in the scope of the entire Bible that a learner needs to advance through the dimensions of the spiritual life to become a mature disciple. For adults this means that all of God's Word needs exploring to gain spiritual insights.

2. Balance—To achieve balance in a curriculum plan means that it has neither overemphasis nor underemphasis of the various parts of the Bible. Appropriate Old and New Testament studies need to be featured.

3. Sequence—This element refers to arranging learning experiences in the best order to meet the needs of the learner. The sequence of units of study in adult Bible study curriculum materials used in the class should take into account the principles of comprehensiveness and balance.

About a decade ago the USDA introduced the food pyramid to train people to develop a healthy, balanced diet of necessary foods. The pyramid recommends servings of foods in five food groups—bread and cereal; vegetables; milk and cheese; meat, poultry, fish, beans, eggs, and nuts; and fruit.

Likewise, a properly developed Bible study curriculum plan represents servings for a healthy spiritual diet. Just as a nutritious and balanced diet requires eating from all food groups, so does appropriate Bible study engage adults to explore all of the Bible.

Making a Personal Connection: Your Resources
Identify the Bible study resources used in your adult Bible study classes.

_____

Why were these materials chosen? What benefits or value do they add to the Bible study experience?

_____

What long-range Bible content areas would you like to study during the next two years? Why does your class need to study these topics or Bible books?

_____

_____

Shaping the Path for Evangelistic
Bible Teaching in an Open Group

Evangelistic Bible teaching through Sunday School provides one of the church's greatest opportunities for reaching secular society. Evangelistic Bible study should permeate the Sunday School experience. The Sunday School exists primarily to reach people for Christ and to help people grow in Christlikeness. More people are won to Christ through the Sunday School class than through any other outreach effort of the church. Why is the Bible study class such an effective means to reach people?

1. Sunday School has the Bible as its textbook and the gospel as its message.
2. Sunday School has evangelistic workers in its organization.
3. Sunday School has the lost in its membership.
4. Sunday School focuses on the personal needs of a common peer group.
5. Sunday School provides evangelistic Bible study resources.

For evangelistic Bible study to happen, an environment for evangelism must be established by the teacher and affirmed by class members through personal relationships, a caring attitude, and the development of witnessing skills necessary to share the gospel during the class setting. Consider these conditions for evangelism that need to take place before, during, and after Bible study.

Before Bible Study
- Encourage the pastor to emphasize evangelism in the church.
- Be involved in evangelistic visitation to establish identity and build a relationship.
- Know the spiritual condition of class members.
- Know how to share your personal testimony about how you came to accept Christ.
- Know how to share the plan of salvation using key Bible verses.
- Enlist a ministry coordinator/visitation-evangelism coordinator to give intentional direction to reaching people.
- Identify the evangelistic potential of the Bible study lesson.
- Pray for lost people in your class by name and ask the Holy Spirit to guide you.
- Invite lost people to class fellowship events.
- Intentionally enroll lost people in the Bible study class.

During Bible Study
- Assume that many people outside the church have little knowledge of the Bible.
- Use easy-to-understand, nonchurch language to explain the gospel.
- Recognize the teaching opportunity when people are under conviction.
- Find natural times during the lesson to explain how to become a Christian

Connecting Sunday School to Life

- Follow up questions learners may ask that suggest a level of interest.
- Regularly explain the plan of salvation.
- Communicate the evangelistic message featured in the Bible passage.
- Use the teaching suggestions to involve people in evangelistic responses.
- Take advantage of lessons specifically tailored to provide an evangelistic thrust.
- Involve class members in explaining how Christ has changed their lives.
- Offer occasions for learners to respond to Christ during class time.

After Bible Study
- Encourage lost people to attend church worship services.
- Express your willingness to "walk the aisle" with an individual during the invitation.
- Be available for people who want to talk to you privately.
- Counsel people who have indicated an interest in accepting Christ.
- Ask the pastor or staff member to make a follow-up visit.
- Celebrate the times when people accept Christ as Savior.

Every Sunday School teacher can be an effective evangelistic teacher by developing these essential characteristics: personal assurance of salvation, a compelling compassion for the lost, a conviction that Christ is the only way to establish a right relationship with God, knowledge of the biblical plan of salvation, a spirit of faithfulness in sharing the gospel, an emphasis on prayer to be sensitive to reaching lost people, and a dependence on the Holy Spirit.

Making a Personal Connection
Identify three ways you could share the gospel during a Bible study class:
1. _____
2. _____
3. _____

Practical Tips for Effective Bible Teaching and Learning in an Open Group
Achieving meaningful results in teaching the Bible requires time, energy, preparation, and sacrifice. An effective teacher understands and practices consistent steps in the Bible teaching process. These 10 steps represent key actions to plan, organize, conduct, and evaluate the Bible study experience.
1. Review the unit and lesson structure.
   - Read the Biblical Truth.
   - Read the Life Impact statement.
2. Read and study the Bible.
   - Read all background and focal passages in the Bible.
   - Summarize the key thrusts of the passage.

- Outline the passage.
- Study the commentary in the learner and leader books.
- Study other Bible resources for additional insights.
- Periodically encourage learners to prepare for the Bible study time by reading the Scriptures and studying the lesson material in advance.

3. Focus on the needs of learners.
- Monitor the levels of the spiritual life among members.
- Identify specific generational and life-stage issues.
- Be sensitive to the ethnic and cultural identity of racial groups.
- Prepare ways to involve members whose primary language is not English.
- Identify the priority needs of each member.
- Review the suggested application ideas in the curriculum materials.
- Pray for each member of your class.

4. Customize your teaching plan.
- Review suggested teaching plan ideas.
- Review the supporting Bible study resources.
- Develop four to six key questions to use to stimulate discussion.
- Organize the Bible study session, department and class periods, to achieve total period teaching in which the entire session relates to the Biblical Truth and moves toward the session Life Impact objective.
- Personalize the teaching steps based on time and space, teaching and learning style preferences, and desired learning objectives.
- Meet regularly with other teachers who use common Bible study materials to review the Scriptures, share teaching ideas, discuss reaching and and witnessing approaches, and pray together.

5. Gather the teaching resources.
- Collect supplies, equipment, or materials.
- Provide writing material and pencils, if needed.
- Prepare assignment information.
- Provide large Bible study maps, as needed.

6. Prepare the physical environment.
- Display visuals and other resources that support the lesson.
- Set up the teaching area arranging chairs, tables, and other equipment.
- Arrange for music and songs.
- Arrive early to prepare any refreshments.

7. Prepare the learning environment.
- Prepare to greet members by name.
- Demonstrate personal concern for each member.
- Welcome visitors.
- Complete records and make announcements.
- Discuss fellowship and outreach plans.

8. Conduct the Bible study.
   • Follow the customized teaching plan.
   • Rely on the Holy Spirit to guide the learning experience.
   • Encourage learners to use their Bibles and their Bible learner guides.
   • Provide opportunities for people to accept Christ.
   • Provide significant time for praying for personal concerns.
   • Distribute devotional and Christian leisure-reading materials.
9. Reach, witness, and care for your members.
   • Counsel people who desire to accept Christ.
   • Contact absentees and prospects.
   • Distribute Bible study resources to absentees and prospects.
10. Evaluate Sunday School work.
   • Evaluate your level of planning.
   • Review the learning environment.
   • Review the level of learner participation and involvement.
   • Identify the successful use of teaching methods.
   • Study enrollment and attendance patterns.
   • Evaluate class relationships.
   • Identify personal leadership training needs.
   • Identify evidences of commitment to Christ.

Making a Personal Connection
What do you consider to be your strength in the teaching process?

In what area do you most need to improve?

Remember how paths are worn from relationships and tell life stories? A well-worn path takes time to emerge. A path is a reflection of what is significant or important in life because the same continuous interactions happen over and over to create the path.

We create spiritual paths too. Spiritual paths are worn from one's relationship with God. A well-worn spiritual path takes a lifetime to emerge. This path is a reflection of what is significant or important in life because continuous interactions with God happen over and over to create the path. Have you helped to create a spiritual path for the learners in your Bible study class?

CHRISTIAN GROWTH STUDY PLAN

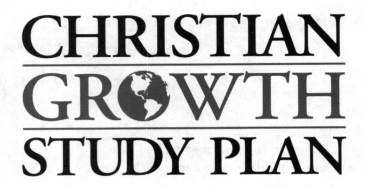

In the **Christian Growth Study Plan (formerly Church Study Course),** *Essentials for Excellence: Connecting Sunday School to Life* is a resource for course credit in one (1) Leadership and Skill Development plan. To receive credit, read the book, complete the learning activities, show your work to your pastor, a staff member or church leader, then complete the following information. This page may be duplicated. Send the completed page to:

Christian Growth Study Plan
One LifeWay Plaza
Nashville, TN 37234-0117
FAX: (615)251-5067
E-mail: *cgspnet@lifeway.com*

For information about the Christian Growth Study Plan, refer to the Christian Growth Study Plan Catalog. It is located online at *www.lifeway.com/cg.* If you do not have access to the Internet, contact the Christian Growth Study Plan office (1.800.968.5519 for the specific plan you need for your ministry.

Essentials for Excellence: Connecting Sunday School to Life
COURSE NUMBER: LS-0048 Developing the Skills of the General Church Leader

PARTICIPANT INFORMATION

Rev. 5-02

Social Security Number (USA Only-optional)	Personal CGSP Number*	Date of Birth (Mo., Day, Yr.)
┃ ┃ ┃ – ┃ ┃ – ┃ ┃ ┃ ┃	┃ ┃ ┃ ┃ – ┃ ┃ ┃ – ┃ ┃ ┃	┃ ┃ – ┃ ┃ – ┃ ┃ ┃

Name (First, MI, Last)	Home Phone
	┃ ┃ ┃ – ┃ ┃ ┃ – ┃ ┃ ┃ ┃

Address (Street, Route, or P.O. Box)	City, State, or Province	Zip/Postal Code

CHURCH INFORMATION

Church Name

Address (Street, Route, or P.O. Box)	City, State, or Province	Zip/Postal Code

CHANGE REQUEST ONLY

☐Former Name		

☐Former Address	City, State, or Province	Zip/Postal Code

☐Former Church	City, State, or Province	Zip/Postal Code

Signature of Pastor, Conference Leader, or Other Church Leader	Date

*New participants are requested but not required to give SS# and date of birth. Existing participants, please give CGSP# when using SS# for the first time. Thereafter, only one ID# is required. *Mail To:* Christian Growth Study Plan, One LifeWay Plaza, Nashville, TN 37234-0117. Fax: (615)251-5067.